Cycling 101

William R. Lamb

Baylor University

Kendall Hunt
publishing company

Cover image © Shutterstock, Inc.

Kendall Hunt
p u b l i s h i n g   c o m p a n y

www.kendallhunt.com
Send all inquiries to:
4050 Westmark Drive
Dubuque, IA 52004-1840

Printed in the United States of America
10 9 8 7 6 5 4 3 2 1

CONTENTS

PREFACE

At a very young age many of us developed a love affair with our bikes. After all, it wasn't just a bike—it was our best friend, our means of escape, our opportunity to fly like a bird, only closer to the ground. Some of our greatest childhood memories involve our bikes. As we got older, however, we replaced our bike with a much faster means of transportation…our first car! We weren't sure where we were going, all we knew was a bicycle wasn't going to get us there fast enough. Once we got that car, there was no time or place in our life for an ordinary bike. Life became simply a race to the finish. **Little did we realize that hurrying to a destination isn't always the best way to get there!** Being reintroduced to bicycling can be a blessing in so many ways. Reaching that destination might take a bit longer but one thing is for sure, the journey will be much more enjoyable.

I've spent the last 30 years as a PGA golf professional. Being an athlete, I have always understood the importance of staying in shape. A healthy diet, weights, and lots of cardio (usually in the form of running or jumping) have been a big part of my life. My joints, however, have asked me to perhaps take it down a notch. I found that biking is an unbelievable way to stay in shape and much more enjoyable than sweating in a gym. One day, my 20-year-old son asked me to ride with him at the wetlands near my home. He said it had some really cool trails that he wanted me to see, so I went. It was fun and quite enjoyable until we had to ride back up the hill to my house. I realized that perhaps biking could replace my workouts, after all, it taxed me more than I thought it would but it really didn't hurt my knees. I had not been on a bike in almost 40 years and then in July of 2011, at age 52, I decided I needed another challenge and biking was it. It has been one of the most rewarding things I have ever done. I now compete in both mountain biking as well as road cycling, and absolutely love riding my bikes anywhere, anytime. Thanks T.

This book was written to provide those interested in taking up cycling with all the general information needed to make cycling a part of their life. I've tried to keep it simple yet informative while providing the information necessary to ride a bike with confidence, a good understanding of the bike itself, and more importantly, to reacquaint those who read it with an old childhood friend. Enjoy the book, enjoy your bike, and enjoy the journey!

William R. Lamb

ACKNOWLEDGMENTS

I would like to thank my son, Trevor, for reintroducing me to biking; Tommy Billeaud aka "coach," for taking me to Cameron Park and trying to kill me; and my wife for not only supporting me, as she always has, but also for allowing me to spend most of our retirement on my bikes. I convinced her that the correct number of bikes for me to own was determined by a simple formula shared with me by my friend Jon at the bike shop. The formula is $(N + 1)$ where "N" represents the current number of bikes owned. She informed me the correct formula was actually $(S - 1)$, where "S" is the number of bikes you could own that would cause your spouse to leave you. Being a mathematician, I've concluded that the perfect number of bikes to own is then defined as $(N = S - 2)$, which is where I stand at the moment. The bike shop does, however, let me keep some bikes at home that are just on loan since I'm such a good customer—that's my story and I'm sticking to it. A special thanks to Ian, Jon, Emilie, Mike, Glenn, Dennis, Paul, Andrew and Fred for their continued support in helping me become a better cyclist by providing me with great equipment, great instruction, as well as a tremendous amount of encouragement, and most of all sharing their passion for this wonderful sport with me.

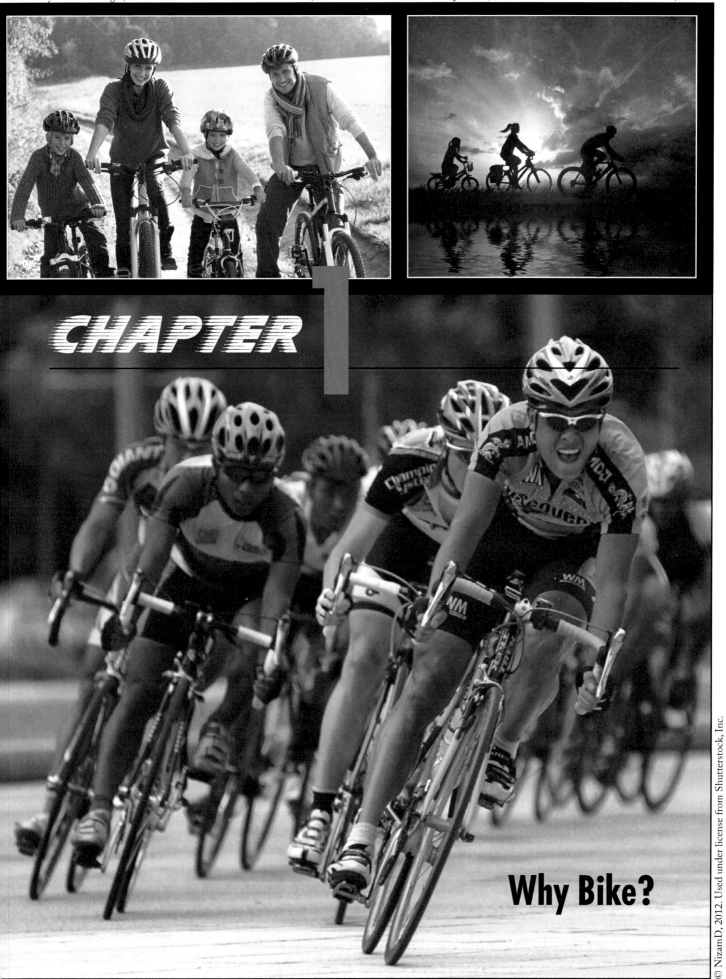

CHAPTER 1

Why Bike?

Why bike? A better question would be, why not? There are a lot of reasons to make riding a bike part of your life. Riding is healthy, it's a great form of stress relief, it's enjoyable, it's an affordable and efficient means of transportation, and biking can allow those of us who need to stay competitive the means to do so. In this chapter we will discuss each of these areas and hopefully it will encourage you to get out there and ride!

ENJOYMENT

Whether riding alone or with friends, bicycling can provide hours of enjoyment. An open road or a winding trail along with a bike tends to bring out the kid in all of us. Cycling allows us to leave the everyday worries behind and chase the adventures that lie ahead. No itinerary, no destination; just an open road, some beautiful scenery, and a gentle breeze. Whether it's just afternoon rides with friends enjoying the camaraderie, a lone trek to clear the mind, or a competitive race; cycling can provide enjoyment for everyone!

STRESS RELIEF

In today's fast-paced society, anything one can do to reduce stress is a good thing. Numerous studies have cited the benefits of exercise on mental health. It is a fact that regular exercise is a great way to reduce stress as well as depression, and improve one's well-being and self esteem. While riding a bicycle, endorphins, a brain chemical that improves our overall mood, are released. The release of these endorphins over time can help us feel good and sleep well, leading to better stress management. Cycling outdoors not only provides exercise but allows us to enjoy nature and to feel the breath of the earth on our faces. It has a way of taking our minds off of everyday-life stress and rejuvenating our souls.

HEALTH BENEFITS

CYCLING IS ONE OF THE EASIEST WAYS TO EXERCISE. You can ride a bicycle almost anywhere, at any time of the year, and without spending a fortune. Many people are afraid of trying certain sports because of the high level of skill that seems to be required, or perhaps because they can't commit to a team sport due to time pressures. Most of us know how to cycle and once you have learned, you don't forget. All you need is a bike, a half an hour here or there when it suits, and a bit of confidence.

CYCLING BUILDS STRENGTH AND INCREASES MUSCLE TONE. Contrary to normal perceptions, cycling is not a fitness activity that solely involves the legs. Cycling builds strength in a holistic manner since every single part of the body is involved. It improves general muscle function gradually, with little risk of over exercise or strain. Regular cycling strengthens leg muscles and is great for the mobility of hip and knee joints. Once you begin to ride on a regular basis, you will start to see a dramatic improvement in the muscle tone of your legs, thighs, rear end and hips, as well as your arms and shoulders.

CYCLING BUILDS STAMINA. Stamina refers to how well you can sustain an effort. Cycling is a good way to build stamina. In fact, it is very effective in doing so. Each ride can be so enjoyable that you fail to notice that you've traveled farther than you did on your last ride.

CYCLING IMPROVES CARDIOVASCULAR FITNESS. Cycling makes the heart pound in a steady manner and studies have shown that regular cycling can increase cardiovascular fitness by 3-7%. Cycling requires the use of the largest muscle group—the legs, thus easily raising one's heart rate. The benefits of this increased heart rate are stamina and fitness.

CYCLING IMPROVES HEART HEALTH. According to the British Medical Association, cycling just 20 miles a week can reduce the risk of coronary heart disease by 50%. A major study of 10,000 civil servants suggested that those who cycled 20 miles over the period of a week were half as likely to suffer heart disease as their non-cycling colleagues.

CYCLING EATS UP CALORIES. Cycling is a good way to lose those unwanted pounds. Steady cycling burns approximately 300 calories per hour. If you cycle for 30 minutes every day, you would burn 11 pounds of fat in a year. Since it helps build muscle, cycling will also boost your metabolic rate long after you've finished your ride.

CYCLING IMPROVES COORDINATION AND BALANCE. Cycling is an activity that involves the whole body. Balancing oneself on a bicycle requires a bit of practice just as maneuvering a bicycle requires some coordination. Therefore, arm-to-leg, feet-to-hands, and body-to-eye coordination are all improved.

TRANSPORTATION

Fitness cycling can really be integrated into any fitness program. With every turn of the wheel, calories are burned, strength is built, and wellness is achieved.

CONSULT YOUR DOCTOR

Most people can do cycling. However, it is always best to consult your doctor when thinking about starting a new activity that involves exercise. They can advise you regarding your limits and capacities and what you should avoid doing.

In the United States, many people still consider cycling only a recreation or professional sport. But millions of Americans have found that cycling is a great way to get to work or get around town. The bicycle is a tremendously efficient means of transportation. **In fact, cycling is more efficient than any other method of travel—including walking!** It takes less energy to bicycle one mile than it takes to walk one mile. A bicycle can be up to 5 times more efficient than walking. The one billion bicycles in the world are a testament to its effectiveness.

According to the Nationwide Personal Transportation Survey (NPTS), bicycling produces multiple potential benefits, both for the individual and their community, and there is a great potential to increase the number of trips taken by bicycle. Approximately 69% of all daily trips are less than five miles, 50% are less than three miles, and 25% are less than one mile (NPTS 1995); well within the range of an average cyclist. It is important to recognize that only 20% of all trips are taken between home and work. The remaining 80% are trips to school, for recreation, and errands (NPTS 1995). The potential for increasing the use of bicycles for these types of trips may be even greater than for commuting, since these trips tend to be shorter distances and can be done in casual clothing.

Until the recent spike in gas prices, much of the discussion about solving our transportation problems—namely, emissions from cars and dependence on foreign oil—centered on increasing

© Mark Bonham, 2012. Used under license from Shutterstock, Inc.

the efficiency of the vehicles we drive through higher CAFE (Corporate Average Fuel Economy) standards and new designs. Let's face it; fancy cars are just sexier than riding a bicycle. Remember, however, that cycling is the most efficient source of transportation. Cycling and energy efficiency are by far the cheapest means of addressing a wide range of issues; from climate change, to congestion, to high energy prices. **Cycling is simply an Overlooked Solution!**

COMPETITIONS

Along with all the above-mentioned benefits, cycling can also help us satisfy those competitive juices. There are many forms of competitive cycling. Within each of these competitions are categories and disciplines designed to help level the playing field. In mountain bike races, for example, there are usually 5 categories: Professional, cat 1, cat 2, cat 3, and single speed. Within each category, with the exception of the professionals, there are disciplines or age groups. This system allows one to compete with others the same age and with similar skill levels. There are several types of cycling competitions, below are a few of the more popular. These competitions will be covered more in-depth in a later chapter.

There are several types of cycling competitions, below are a few of the more popular ones. These competitions will be covered more in-depth in a later chapter.

Crit or Criterium

A bike race held on a short course (usually less than 5 km), often run on closed-off city center streets.

Road Race

A bicycle racing sport held on roads, using racing bicycles. The term "road racing" is usually applied to events where competing riders start simultaneously (unless riding a handicap event) with the winner being the first to the line at the end of the course.

Time Trials

A road bicycle race in which cyclists race alone against the clock (in French: *contre la montre*—literally "against the watch," in Italian: *tappa a cronometro*—"stopwatch stage").

Mountain Bike Racing

The Union Cycliste Internationale (UCI) recognized the sport of **mountain bike racing** relatively late in 1990, when it sanctioned the world championships in Purgatory, Colorado. The National Off-Road Bicycle Association, commonly known as NORBA, was formed in the early months of 1983. It had become evident as the number of riders grew at every race, that if mountain bike racing were to expand beyond a few races among friends, a consistent set of rules and insurance to protect promoters would be necessary. If a national championship were ever to be awarded, some national organization had to exist in order to declare a champion.

Cycle Cross

Races typically take place in the autumn and winter (the international or "World Cup" season is September–January), and consists of many laps of a short (2.5–3.5 km or 1.5–2 mile) course featuring pavement, wooded trails, grass, steep hills, and obstacles requiring the rider to quickly dismount, carry the bike whilst navigating the obstruction and remount.

WHY BIKE CHAPTER TEST

1. List 3 reasons to make riding a bike part of your life.

   _____, _____, _____

2. List 3 health benefits of riding a bike.

   _____, _____, _____

3. Cycling is more efficient than any other means of travel, even more so than walking.

   ____True   ____False

4. Steady cycling burns approximately how many calories per hour? _____

5. In mountain bike racing, there are usually 5 categories; name them. _____,

   _____, _____, _____, _____

6. Categories are further split up into age groups known as _____.

7. List 5 different types of competitions. _____,_____,

   _____, _____, _____

8. What does NORBA refer to? _____

   _____

9. What does UCI stand for? _____ _____ _____

10. What percent of all daily trips are less than 5 Miles? _____

CHAPTER 2

Choosing a Bike

When I was growing up, a bike was a bike. The choices were pretty simple, you got a girl's bike or a boy's bike and not much more. Bicycling has come a long way over the past two decades and now there are bikes designed for virtually every circumstance imaginable. Bikes are separated into basically five categories, mountain bikes, road bikes, hybrids, cruisers, and specialty bikes such as stunt and racing bikes.

TYPES OF BIKES

Mountain bikes are designed to be very effective in handling off-road circumstances. They usually have a higher clearance, much bigger tires, and some type of suspension. They are designed to climb and descend over very rough terrain.

Road bikes are designed to be very effective when you're riding on smooth surfaces, such as highways, with little or no obstacles. They are lower, have a more aerodynamic feel, and have extremely small tires.

Hybrids are designed to do a little of both. They are rugged enough to go off road but are streamlined enough to ride on smooth surfaces as well.

Cruisers are strictly for doing just what they suggest—cruising! They are very comfortable bikes designed to allow your ride, whether a commute or just-for-fun ride, to be as comfortable as possible. Cruisers have a larger, softer seat, allow you to sit more upright, and generally have a means of carrying belongings such as a front basket.

Specialty bikes are bikes that are designed for a specific purpose such as performing stunts or racing. These bikes take a form of the above mentioned bikes and modify them to fit the need of the sport they are being used for.

CHOOSING THE RIGHT BIKE FOR YOU

Since good bicycles are rather expensive, it is usually not feasible to buy more than one or two bikes at the most. When choosing a bike, one should carefully consider what their primary use of the bike will be. For example, if you are purchasing a bike to only commute back and forth to work and your route will be on smooth surfaces, then a mountain bike would totally be the wrong choice; but a cruiser or a road bike would work great.

The truth is, many people want to use their bike for multiple purposes. They want to commute to and from places but in doing so, they may have to cross grass areas or travel on some trails. For this reason a hybrid is a great choice for the average biker. Hybrids are nimble enough for highways yet rugged enough for trails and most of all, saves from having to buy and store two bikes.

https://www.youtube.com/watch?edit=vd&v=fprAO_RjSyQ

CHOOSING A BIKE CHAPTER TEST

1. Name the five categories that bikes are separated into.

   _____, _____, _____,

   _____, _____

2. Which bike is designed rugged enough to go off-road, but streamlined enough to ride on smooth surfaces?

   _____

3. When choosing a bike, what is the first thing a person should consider?

   _____

   _____

4. What type of bike would you choose if you were looking for a bike that handled well off-road as well as be able to climb and descend over rough terrain?

   _____

5. What specific purposes are specialty bikes designed for?

   _____

6. If you want a very comfortable bike, that allows you to carry your belongings, what type of bike would be a good choice?

   _____

7. What are two characteristics that road bikes have which make them very effective when riding on roads/highways with few obstacles?

   _____

   _____

   _____

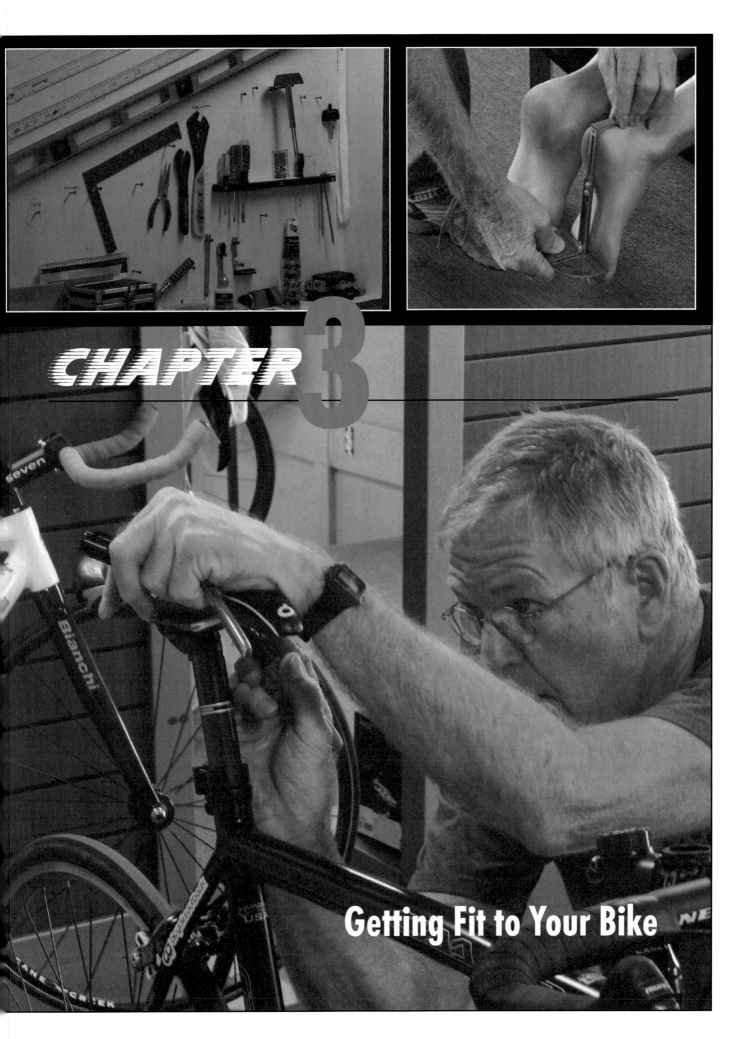

CHAPTER 3

Getting Fit to Your Bike

IMPORTANCE OF A PROPER FIT

Perhaps the most important aspect of selecting a new bike is achieving the right fit. It's fun to discuss the benefits of a carbon bike vs. an aluminum bike, as well as the road tests and race wins—but the reality is that one thing matters more than anything else: when you select your new bike, it needs to fit you! Obtaining the proper fit allows the cyclist to be more efficient, more comfortable, and riding itself much more enjoyable.

An improper bike fit can cause serious discomfort including things such as a numbing of the bum and feet, knee or back pain, sore hands, achy shoulders and a stiff neck. While the information below can be very useful to make minor adjustments to your bike fit, I highly recommend that you take the time and spend the money to have your bike professionally fit. In the long run, the extra expense will be more than worth it.

BASIC OR HARD FIT

The following information is simply a way for you to hard-fit yourself to your bike. The stand over fit will help you determine what size bike to by. Once the bike is purchased, the remaining steps will help you fit the bike to yourself.

STAND-OVER HEIGHT: While straddling the bike, place one hand on the handle bar and one hand on the back of the saddle. Raise the bike until it makes contact with the crotch. For a road bike, the tires should be between 1-2 inches above the ground. For a mountain bike, perhaps 3-4 inches above the ground.

You will need a bicycle trainer and a friend to complete the rest of the process. Start by placing your bike in a trainer. Next get on your bike and pedal for a short while to loosen up.

SADDLE HEIGHT: With crank arms parallel to the seat tube, raise or lower the saddle to allow the bend in the extended leg to be between 10 and 20 degrees.

SADDLE POSITION: With the crank arms parallel to the ground, drop a plumb line from the bottom of the knee cap down through the pedals. This line should bisect the pedal axle. Adjust the saddle forward or aft until the plumb line bisects the pedal axle. Also, always start with the saddle as level as possible. After you have had some time on the bike, you may find that moving the nose of the saddle up or down is better for you but level is a good starting place.

HORIZONTAL BODY POSITION: This is the most important adjustment for establishing comfort. Begin by placing your hands on top of the brake hoods. From this position, sight the front hub relative to the handlebar. The handlebar should obscure the front hub. If the handlebar is in front of the hub, you will need a slightly shorter stem and if the handlebar is behind the hub, you will need a slightly longer stem. This should put your back at about a 45-degree angle.

HANDLEBAR WIDTH: Generally speaking, the handlebars should be about as wide as your shoulders. A wider handlebar will help to open up your diaphragm while a narrower handlebar will make you more aerodynamic.

CLEAT POSITION: In general, the center of the cleat should be directly under the ball of your foot.

Getting your shoes and feet set up properly has a profound effect on how you perform on your bike. Having them set up improperly can lead not only to a lack of efficiency, but injuries throughout your body as well.

The above guide aims to get you to a good starting place and small adjustments may be necessary after some time on your bike. Keep in mind that the most important thing to consider when fitting your bicycle is comfort.

WHERE DO I GET PROFESSIONALLY FIT?

Although a hard-fit can get your bike and you closer to being one, as I said before, it is definitely worth the money to get professionally fit. A good quality bike shop is a must if you're going to spend much time on a bike. Many quality shops have full-time fitters and a full-time fitter is always preferred to an employee that has, as one of his duties, to hard-fit clients.

You can have your bike fit at any reputable bike shop but keep in mind, some fitters are much better at what they do than others. It's best to do a little research and find a fitter that has a wealth of experience and a good reputation in the bicycle community. Start by contacting your local bicycle club and talking to some of the riders to see who they might recommend. You can also search the Internet for fitters in your area. A quality fitter can make riding your bike go from not-bad to *amazing*!

https://www.youtube.com/watch?v=iwFNYe6N1xs

GETTING FIT TO YOUR BIKE
CHAPTER TEST

1. Obtaining the proper fit allows the cyclist to be _____, _____, and makes the ride itself more _____.

2. List 3 things that can be caused by an improper fit. _____ _____
   _____

3. The stand-over height for a properly fit road bike should place the tires _____inches above the ground as opposed to a mountain bike which would be _____ inches above the ground.

4. When the saddle height is adjusted properly, the extended leg should have an angle between _____and _____ degrees.

5. When using a plumb line to ensure that the knee is in the correct position in reference to the pedal axle, what part of the bike are we adjusting? _____
   _____

6. When part of the bike can be changed to adjust the horizontal body position _____
   _____.

7. Generally speaking, the correct handlebar width should be approximately _____
   _____.

8. When your cleats are fit properly, the ball of the foot should be directly over the center of the cleat, true or false? _____

9. Where is a good place to start when looking for a professional fitter? _____
   _____

CHAPTER 4

Clothing and Accessories

CLOTHING AND ACCESSORIES

Clothing and accessories play a huge role in all types of cycling. Not only do they ensure your safety and well-being but they also help make your biking experience fun, enjoyable, and comfortable.

CYCLING SHORTS

Cycling shorts are very helpful in that they have a pad sewn into the saddle area that helps to reduce the soreness that comes with spending a good deal of time on a bike. These shorts come in a variety of styles, from skin tight with no pockets to baggy and full of pockets. I certainly feel more comfortable in the baggy shorts but they can prove to be a nuisance when getting on and off your bike. When wearing biking shorts, you should not wear undergarments.

CYCLING SHIRTS

Cycling shirts are also very helpful as they have much needed pockets on the back. These pockets allow you to carry food and supplies that are easily assessable while riding. They, too, come in a wide variety of styles, colors, and materials. Generally speaking, if you are racing, the fit is usually quite tight to help with aerodynamics. The materials are designed to keep you dry by wicking away moisture.

CYCLING SHOES (TYPES OF CLIPS)

1 SPD

2 Time

3 Speedplay

4 Eggbeater

5 Look

6 Shimano Ultegra

The pedals on your bike really serve only one purpose—a means to transfer power from you to your bicycle. For riding around the block, they don't need to be very fancy... just plastic blocks with grooves or teeth to plant your feet onto. But if you want to go on longer rides (anything over 10 miles), you'll benefit greatly from something better, because:

- Without something holding your foot securely to the pedal, it would be easy to slip off the pedal and send your foot into the wheel or ground. Not so likely to happen on a trip around the block; but on a longer ride, when you're tired.
- There is a correct placement for the position of your foot over the pedal axle.
- A good pedal/shoe system has to be able to transfer all of the power from your leg to the pedals without trying to bend your foot over the top of the pedal, which causes both fatigue and pain.
- You shouldn't have to think about how your feet connect to the bicycle while you're riding. You should be concentrating on having fun! With a clipless pedal system, you wear special cycling shoes that allow a "cleat" to be mounted to their sole. This cleat literally snaps into a receptacle on the pedal, allowing you to quickly (and without having to reach down!) connect your shoes to the pedals as well as remove them from the pedals. Your pedal efficiency is greater using clipless pedals as you are able not only to push down on your pedal, but to pull up as well and thereby increase power efficiency by up to 30%, not to mention allowing different muscle groups to share the work. The type of bike you ride will determine the type of pedal you'll use. SPD type pedals work better with mountain bikes since the cleat is recessed into the bottom of the shoe, allowing you to walk when necessary. Look-style pedals use cleats that are mounted to the bottom of the shoe and are designed for road bikes. This type of pedal simply doesn't work for mountain bikers who need to get off their bike and walk or run at times.

CYCLING HELMETS

Cycling helmets are a must as far as I'm concerned. In 95-97% of all biking fatalities, the biker was not wearing a helmet. When it comes to choosing a helmet, the first order of business is to make sure you purchase one that is **CPSC** (Consumer Product Safety Commission) approved.

- **Find the right style.** Cycling helmets come in 3 basic styles—sport, road, and mountain bike helmets. All types are designed to protect riders from impact while being light, comfortable, and stylish.
- **Find the right size.** To determine your size, wrap a flexible tape measure around the largest portion of your head—about 1 inch above your eyebrows. Or, wrap a string or ribbon around your head, then measure the length of string with a straight-edge ruler or yardstick. Look for a helmet that matches your measurement.
- **Adjust the fit.** You want the helmet touching your head all the way around. It should be snug and secure but comfortable. It should sit level so that the top of the helmet comes off your forehead at a 90-degree angle. It should be no more than an inch over your eyebrows and just barely visible to you when you are wearing it. After correctly fitting the helmet, shake your head vigorously and be sure it stays snug and secure.

CYCLING GLOVES

Cycling gloves come in a very wide variety of styles from fully enclosed to fingerless, from extremely padded to very thin. Gloves are designed for the different needs of cyclists. For example, mountain bike gloves can be designed to help protect the rider's hands where as road bike gloves may be designed more toward keeping the hands comfortable.

© iStockphoto/Thinkstock

© Radu Razvan, 2012. Used under license from Shutterstock, Inc.

© vlad_star, 2012. Used under license from Shutterstock, Inc.

Cycling gloves do a few basic things:

- They reduce friction between your hands and the handle bars
- They dampen vibrations which might cause hand/finger numbness
- They reduce pressure on the ulna nerve, which can also cause numbness
- In summer months they keep your hands dry, ensuring a good grip on the handlebars
- Some designs help provide protection, especially for mountain bikers
- Although most do not, they can provide warmth if equipped with an inner layer making them windproof.

CYCLING EYEWEAR

© Oleg Zabielin, 2012. Used under license from Shutterstock, Inc.

© Maciej Oleksy, 2012. Used under license from Shutterstock, Inc.

© spe, 2012. Used under license from Shutterstock, Inc.

Cycling eyewear is a must when riding a bike. Your bike doesn't have a windshield to protect you from debris such as rocks or insects. The last thing you want is to get hit in the eye while riding your bike. Your first reaction will be to grab your eye, which means letting go of the handlebars … not good. It is best to get eyewear that has a relatively clear lens. If you get caught after dark with a darker lens, it will be necessary to remove the eyewear to see, thus leaving your eyes unprotected. Most cycling glasses now are available with interchangeable lenses, which is a real plus.

HYDRATION

Staying hydrated while you ride is very important. There are several ways to accomplish this. The old standby has always been just a water bottle that can be carried in the pocket on the back of your cycling shirt or in a cage mounted to the frame of your bike. Hydration packs are basically the newest craze and consist of a water bladder inside of a back pack with a tube that runs to the front of the pack. Hydration packs have many advantages over the water bottle:

- **Portability** – Hydration packs fit over both shoulders, freeing the hands to maneuver a bicycle. Where multiple water bottles fill the pockets or take up valuable bag or hand space, the hydration pack features a self-contained bladder.

- **Capacity** – Since the bladder size can vary greatly, the hydration pack allows a rider to choose a pack to fit his or her personal needs.
- **Convenience** – Convenience and safety contribute to an effective workout. Hydration packs contain a mouthpiece connected to the bladder by a length of hose. The design allows for hands-free operation. The feature proves particularly beneficial for such activities as cycling since the rider does not have to reach down and retrieve as well as replace a water bottle.
- **Cargo Space** – For some outdoor enthusiasts, the list of "things to bring" contains more than just "water." Hydration packs containing pockets and zippers allow a cyclist, for instance, to stow a spare inner tube or to pack lunch.

The downside to hydration packs is that they are weight on your back. When you carry extra weight on your back, sometimes your neck and shoulders will get tight or sore. Today's hydration packs are much improved over those of the past. Some now have the bladder around the lower portion of the back which places the weight in a more manageable position. They also range from very small to very large, depending on what your need is.

LIGHTS, TOOLS, AND REPAIR EQUIPMENT

When you ride your bike, you should always be prepared for the unexpected. Carrying some basic safety and repair tools is a must. You should have a light in case you find yourself in a situation where you are on your bike after dark (not recommended). The tools and supplies necessary to repair a flat: a spare tube, a way to inflate that tube such as a small pump or a CO_2 cartridge, a tire tool, a patch kit, and perhaps an extra master link for your chain. These items will all fit in a small pouch that can be stored in the back pockets of your cycling shirt or in a seat bag. Pushing your bike is much harder than riding it!

© Roblan, 2012. Used under license from Shutterstock, Inc.
Bicycle tire pump

© Winai Tepsuttinun, 2012. Used under license from Shutterstock, Inc.
Bicycle light

© Jim Hughes, 2012. Used under license from Shutterstock, Inc.
Bicycle tire repair kit

© iStockphoto/Thinkstock
Tube

© Olga Popova, 2012. Used under license from Shutterstock, Inc.
Bicycle tool

© Jiri Pavlik, 2012. Used under license from Shutterstock, Inc.
Bicycle seat bag

TRANSPORTING YOUR BIKE

From time to time you'll need to transport your bike from one place to another. There are several types of bike racks that are available to assist you. Below are a few examples.

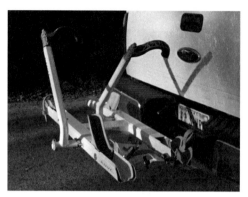

Hitch racks

Roof racks

Trunk racks

Bed racks

Remember when purchasing a bicycle rack to make sure you get one that will work with your vehicle and have your local bicycle shop install it. When you get where you are going, you will be disappointed if your bike isn't there with you!

Name _____ Section _____

CLOTHING AND ACCESSORIES CHAPTER TEST

1. Why do cycling shorts have a pad sewn into the saddle area? _____
   _____

2. Why are pockets placed in the back of a cycling shirt? _____
   _____

3. What is the main purpose of a bike pedal? _____
   _____

4. When choosing a bike helmet, be sure purchase one that is _____
   approved.

5. List the three steps that will help you choose the right bike helmet for you.
   _____
   _____
   _____

6. List two benefits of bicycle gloves. _____
   _____
   _____

7. What could happen if you choose not to wear protective eyewear while cycling? _____
   _____
   _____

8. What are two items that you can use to stay hydrated on a ride?
   _____

9. What bicycle equipment might you need if you find yourself riding after dark? _____
   _____

Clothing and Accessories --- 29

CHAPTER 5

Anatomy of a Bike

1 _____

2 _____

3 _____

4 _____

5 _____

6 _____

7 _____

8 _____

9 _____

10 _____

11 _____

12 _____

13 _____

14 _____

15 _____

16 _____

17 _____

18 _____

19 _____

20 _____

a) Break Lines

b) Break Levers

c) Chain

d) Chain Stay

e) Crank Arm

f) Crank Set

g) Down Tube

h) Front Fork

i) Hub

j) Rear Cassette

k) Rear Derailleur

l) Rim

m) Saddle

n) Seat Collar

o) Seat Post

p) Seat Stay

q) Spoke

r) Tire

s) Top Tube

t) Valve

It is important that you not only can identify the parts of your bike but also that you understand how they work both individually and as a unit. The more familiar we are with how our bikes work, the more competent we become in riding them.

Some of the first bikes, known as Penny Farthing bikes, had a really big wheel in the front and a really small wheel in the back. They worked like a child's tricycle in that the pedals were connected to the front wheel. Every revolution of the pedals meant one revolution of the wheel. This presented a problem of sorts. Imagine pedaling a tricycle with a very small wheel. The upside would be that pedaling would require little effort; the downside would be that pedaling as fast as you could, would only result in a speed of about 2 mph. If the wheel were bigger, you could go much faster but pedaling would require much more effort. Since roads are not flat, the size of the wheel would become extremely important. Going uphill, you would need a really small wheel or turning the pedals would require a tremendous amount of strength. Going downhill, you would need a much larger wheel or you couldn't keep your feet on the pedals due to their speed.

The modern bicycle addresses the problem by introducing gears. Gears basically allow us to change the "size" of our wheels without actually changing our wheels. Today's bicycles have two wheels similar in size, connected by a frame. The pedals are connected to chain rings and form a unit called a **crank set** that is connected to the frame and not the wheels. A set of different sized gears referred to as cogs, make up a unit called the **rear cassette,** which is connected to the rear wheel hub. The crank set and the rear cassette are connected to each other by a device referred to as a **chain**. By connecting different cogs in the back to different chain rings, you can effectively change the size of the bicycles wheels. A combination of a big chain ring and a small cog basically results in the bike having a big wheel, difficult to turn but capable of high speeds. A combination of a small chain ring and a big cog basically results in the bike having a small wheel—it won't produce much speed but it's quite easy to turn. A device known as a **front derailleur** moves the chain from one chain ring to another whereas a device known as a **rear derailleur** moves the chain from one cog to another. **Shifters** on the handle bars move the derailleurs, the shifter on the left moves the front and the shifter on the right moves the back.

Understanding exactly how the gears accomplish this feat requires a bit of physics and since this is Cycling 101, we will leave that to the next book. Just remember the Penny Farthing, in that it had a big wheel on the front and a small wheel on the back and was hard to pedal. So when you're in a big chain ring on the front and a small cog on the back, the combination will look like that bike of old and… it's going to be hard to pedal!

Modern bikes also have a much improved method of stopping. Unlike bikes of old where you basically had to stop pedaling and then push backwards on the pedals, today's bikes have brakes on each wheel. The brakes in the front are controlled by the brake lever on the left and the brakes in the back by the lever on the right. In many cases, the brake and derailleur levers are built together. If the lever is pushed side-to-side, it moves the derailleur and if it is compressed, it works the brakes. There are basically 4 different types of brakes: **cantilever, disc, caliber,** and **center pull**. The type of brakes used on a bike is determined by whether the bike is to be used on pavement or off-road. Disc brakes are the strongest type of brake, and for that reason they're popular on mountain, touring, and cyclocross bikes where stopping can be harder than on normal surfaces or with normal carried weight. These brakes also work well regardless of weather conditions, but they're expensive and heavy. Their weight makes them undesirable for road bikes. Caliper brakes are the most common type of brake used on road bikes, particularly models made before the 1990s. This brake uses an arched or horseshoe-shaped bracket to hold the brake pads near the wheel rim, and pivot joints on the bracket move when the brake cable is tightened to draw the pads onto the wheel rim.

The only other piece of important information that you need to know about how your bike works is that momentum can be your best friend or your worst enemy. Since you only have two wheels, momentum is a necessity in keeping you and your bike upright. By the same token, you only have two wheels so any change in momentum, if not calculated, can be somewhat unpleasant. For example, if you accidentally grab your front brakes while traveling at a high speed the momentum caused by the sudden movement of your weight forward could send you over the handlebars—not a lot of fun!

http://youtu.be/U9JZV_KeBxM

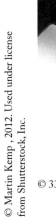

© Martin Kemp , 2012. Used under license from Shutterstock, Inc.

© 3355m, 2012. Used under license from Shutterstock, Inc.

Two styles of valves are found on bicycle tubes, the presta valve on the left and the schrader valve on the right.

© hamurishi, 2012. Used under license from Shutterstock, Inc.

© maga, 2012. Used under license from Shutterstock, Inc.

Bicycle tires are available from super slicks to extremely knobby.

Cranksets consist of 1, 2, or 3 chain rings, and 2 crank arms.

Cassettes are the sets of sprockets mounted on the hub of the rear wheel.

Bicycle seats, commonly referred to as saddles, come in many different sizes and shapes. Some are designed for aerodynamics and others for comfort.

© Dmitry Naumov, 2012. Used under license from Shutterstock, Inc.

© Dmitry Naumov, 2012. Used under license from Shutterstock, Inc.

Front and rear derailleurs move the chain from one chain ring to another or from one cog to another. The rear (left) moves the cogs and the front (right) moves the chain rings.

© Thomas Northcut/Photodisc/Thinkstock

Bicycle wheel, spokes, and hub.

The three most common styles of bicycle brakes are Disc (left), Caliber (middle), and Cantilever (right).

The three most common styles of bicycle handlebars are Tri-bars (left), Road (middle), and Mountain (right).

Bicycle handlebars consist of three main areas, the hoods (left), the tops (middle), and the drops (right).

Bicycle shifters come in a variety of styles depending on the type bicycle you have.

Bicycle forks basically serve as shocks.

ANATOMY OF A BIKE CHAPTER TEST

1. _____ allow a cyclist to change the size of the bike's wheels without changing the actual wheels.

2. The pedals are connected to chain rings and form a unit called a _____

   _____.

3. What are the four types of bicycle brakes? _____

   _____

   _____

   _____

4. Which type of brake is most commonly used on road bikes? _____

   _____

5. Which device moves the chain from one chain ring to another? _____

   _____

6. Which device moves the chain from one cog to another? _____

   _____

7. The shifter on the left controls which derailleur? _____

   _____

8. What is absolutely necessary to keep you and your bike upright? _____

   _____

CHAPTER 6

Maintenance and Repair

IMPORTANCE OF MAINTENANCE

Bicycles are complex pieces of equipment. They have a lot more going on than meets the eye. A well maintained bike can provide you with safe and reliable service for many years. Even if your bike is performing flawlessly, you should schedule routine maintenance checkups. This will allow you to catch a potential problem before it becomes an actual problem. These checkups should be performed by a certified bike mechanic and not just Uncle Bob, even if he is good with lawn mowers!

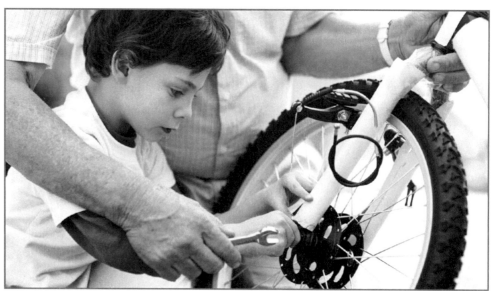

TOOLS AND SUPPLIES

You will need a few supplies to perform routine maintenance on your bike.

- Bucket
- Soft bristle brush, sponge, and tooth brush
- Soft cloth for drying
- Tire pump with gauge
- Tire tool
- A dry or wet lube (examples of dry lube: White Lightning, wet lube: TriFlow)
- A Teflon-based spray lube for derailleurs
- Bike tool

BASIC MAINTENANCE

- Keep your bike dry. Keep your bike inside if you can, to avoid exposure to water which will rust moving parts. If this is not possible, consider buying a cover.
- Keep your bike clean. This prolongs its life. Pay particular attention to the moving parts which will rust if left dirty. Do not use soap and water as this can leave a salty residue causing corrosion. Just use a damp cloth or if your bike is really dirty, use specialist bike cleaning liquid.
- Lubricate the chain and pedals. This will keep them working properly and reduce wear and tear. Use a specialist bike lubricant which helps clean and protect. Hold a cloth underneath to catch any excess. Do this about once a week. Don't allow the lubricant to get onto the brakes or pedals as this will stop them from working properly.
- Check the tires. Tires should be fully inflated before you ride. Under-inflated tires will tend to cause uneven wear and are more susceptible to pinch flats. The correct pressure is written on the side of the tire. Tires can lose up to 5% of their pressure per day so always check them.

http://www.youtube.com/watch?v=vMpjHRXL9RY

TIRE REPAIR

It's much harder to explain to a person how to repair a tire then it is to show them how to repair it. For that reason I have decided to use QR Codes. Scan the QR code and it will take you to a video that will show you step-by-step how to take a tire off the wheel, repair or replace the tube, and remount the tire. Or manually go to the link on your computer.

http://www.youtube.com/watch?v=eT-vDXQXtRA

CHAIN REPAIR

Same goes for a chain, enjoy!

http://www.youtube.com/watch?v=mhYEia3ByUU

MAINTENANCE AND REPAIR
CHAPTER TEST

1. Bicycle checkups should be done by a _____
   _____.

2. Why is it important to keep your bike inside or covered? _____
   _____

3. Never allow lubricant to get onto the _____ or
   _____ as this will stop them from working properly.

4. Tires can lose up to _____ of their pressure per day.

5. Under inflated tires can cause uneven _____ and are more
   susceptible to pinch _____ _____.

6. List 3 items that are needed to perform routine maintenance on your bike. _____
   _____
   _____

7. True or False (Circle one.) If your bike seems to be performing flawlessly, you can skip
   any necessary maintenance until you think something might be wrong.

8. What's the first thing you should do before placing the new tube in the tire? _____
   _____
   _____

9. To repair a broken chain you will need a chain tool and a _____
   _____.

CHAPTER 7

Safety

BASIC SAFETY RULES

It is possible to have mishaps when riding a bike just as one does when driving a car, and yes, some can be serious. Following some basic safety rules, however, can help keep those mishaps to a minimum. Below is a list of some basic rules you can follow to help ensure that riding will be a safe and enjoyable experience.

Inspect your bike before each ride

1. Check to see if the tires are inflated to the proper tire pressure
2. Check the brakes to make sure they are in good working condition
3. Check the wheels' quick release levers to ensure that they are tight

Wear the proper attire

1. Always wear a helmet (95-97% of all cyclists who die in crashes were not wearing a helmet)
2. If you wear pants as opposed to cycling shorts, make sure you wear a trouser clip or band to keep the pant leg from getting caught in the chain rings
3. Dress appropriately for the expected weather conditions
4. If you wear shoes with laces, make sure the laces are tucked in the top of the shoe
5. Make sure your clothing is bright and highly visible
6. When biking at night, wear reflective clothing and use lights

Practice your basic skills

1. Practice getting on and off your bike
2. Practice starting and stopping
3. Practice looking over your shoulder while maintaining a straight path

Choose a safe route

1. Avoid heavily traveled areas as often as possible
2. When choosing a route, take into consideration the type of road surface, elevation changes, major intersections, construction, and surroundings
3. Avoid choosing a route that takes you through a troubled part of town with a high crime rate

Be aware of potentially dangerous road hazards

1. Sand, gravel, and water provide horrible traction and can easily cause a loss of control
2. Railroad tracks, rumble strips, pot holes, or buckling can unexpectedly jolt you causing you to lose control of your bike

Avoid distractions

1. Never wear headphones while riding
2. Never use a telephone while riding
3. Never text while riding

Obey traffic laws

1. Ride your bike as if you were driving a car
2. Use proper hand signals when turning, slowing, or stopping
3. Never ride against traffic
4. Never ride on sidewalks
5. Stay as far right as possible when riding in traffic except when facing an intersection
6. Safely take the middle of the lane when passing through an intersection and then move back to the right
7. Never allow yourself to be put in between two cars or a car and a curb

Know your limits

1. Have a realistic sense of your skill level and ride accordingly
2. Start with short rides and build to identify distances you are comfortable with as well as supplies needed (water and food)
3. Never be ashamed to get off your bike and walk to avoid an uncomfortable situation

http://www.youtube.com/watch?v=5WFgaBXOqVg

EXPECT THE UNEXPECTED

Being prepared for the unexpected is a must in cycling. While riding a bike, you are not as well protected as you would be in your automobile and thus, should take a much closer look at your surroundings. Animals, weather, traffic, and time of day can provide real challenges if not taken in consideration before a ride. Taking the time to pre-ride a desired route is highly suggested. Do the pre-ride during the hours that you are considering and remember to take into consideration that it will take longer on a bike.

Animals – Animals are more of a safety challenge than one may think, especially dogs.

1. If possible, pre-ride your bike routes in your car, making notes of possible trouble areas
2. Firmly shout "NO" to dogs before they get close to you
3. Prepare to give the dog a squirt in his face with your water bottle
4. Never kick at a dog—it will only slow you down or agitate the dog more

Weather – Weather conditions can deteriorate rapidly and can have a devastating effect on your ride.

1. Rain can make the pavement slippery
2. Wind can slow your pace as much as 80%
3. Both wind and rain can cause your trip to take much longer than expected
4. Longer trips could leave you without proper nutrition or clothing
5. Longer trips can put you in driving conditions you weren't prepared for (darkness, rush-hour, etc.)

Traffic – It is quite difficult to anticipate what drivers may do, but we must try.

1. Always ride as if you were driving an automobile
2. Follow traffic laws
3. Remember you are harder to see than an automobile, be as visible as possible
4. Take the middle of the lane at intersections, never get caught between the traffic and the curb
5. Be prepared when passing parked cars for opening doors, sudden movements back into traffic, etc.

Group Rides – Riding with a group can be a lot of fun but also a bit dangerous.

1. Be consistent in speed and positioning
2. Signal riders behind you of upcoming road conditions, pot holes, cracks, etc.
3. Signal riders behind you of upcoming maneuvers such as slowing, stopping, and turning
4. Never ride more than two abreast unless the road is closed to traffic and avoid swerving as much as possible

BICYCLE SECURITY

It is estimated that almost a half million bicycles are stolen in the United States each year. In 1996, according to the FBI Uniform Crime Report, bicycle theft was the only larceny category that increased. More than 1,300 bicycles are stolen in the U.S. each day, valued at an average of $252. The total value of nearly 500,000 bikes stolen annually is $126 million. Most bicycles are stolen from the home. For many of us, our bike is more than just an investment. Whether it cost $50 or $5,000, it's ours and we would like to keep it that way. A bicycle represents a substantial investment and is a popular item of theft. Engraving and registering your bike helps protect the bike and serves as a deterrent to would-be bike thieves. It also helps the police in identifying and returning a found or stolen bike to the owner.

LOCKING YOUR BICYCLE

When unattended, bicycles should *always* be locked. U-shaped bar and shackle locks are the most effective devices for preventing bicycle theft. Its efficient design and solid construction makes it difficult to defeat by pry bars, hammers, freezing, hacksaws, and bolt cutters.

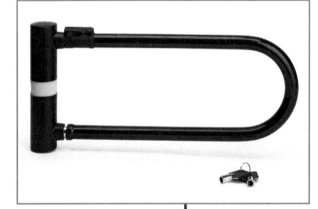

© Dorling Kindersley RF/Thinkstock

- For bicycles with quick-release front wheels, remove the front wheel and place the bike against a stationary object such as a bike rack. Then, take the front wheel and place it next to the rear wheel. Place the U-bar around the bike rack and the bike seat tube and through the two wheels. Attach the crossbar and lock it.
- For bicycles with bolt-on front wheels, place the U-bar around the bike rack and down tube, and through the front wheel. Use a cable lock for extra protection.

http://youtube.com/watch?v=8c5vBpY8SVI

SAFETY CHAPTER TEST

1. List 3 things you should check on your bike before a ride._____
   _____

2. List 3 potentially dangerous road hazards. _____
   _____

3. You should always ride against traffic.   True or False

4. What percentage of bicycle fatalities involve cyclists who were not wearing a helmet:
   _____%

5. When approaching an intersection, a cyclist should always stay as close to the curb as
   possible. True or False

6. Cyclists must follow the same laws as motor vehicles.   True or False

7. List 3 things a cyclist should take into consideration when planning a route. _____
   _____
   _____

8. List 2 ways weather conditions can affect your ride. _____
   _____

9. When possible, a cyclist should pre-ride a desired route. List 2 pieces of information
   that can be obtained by a pre-ride. _____
   _____

10. Approximately how many bicycles are stolen each day in the United States?
    _____

CHAPTER 8

Rules of the Road

Rules are simply a part of life, some we like and some we don't. When it comes to riding a bike, just as with an automobile, there are rules we must follow. These rules are intended to help keep cyclists as safe as possible. Understanding the rules is quite simple; when riding your bike, think of yourself as the operator of a motor vehicle. *You're driving a car, only it looks like a bike*! The relationship between cyclists and automobile drivers is touchy to say the least and as a cyclist, it is imperative that we do our part to make it better. The best way to accomplish that goal is to follow the rules and be as courteous as possible in doing so.

THE OPEN ROAD

The open road is a beautiful place but it's also a dangerous place. As cyclists, we understand that we have rights as well as responsibilities. We should treat motorists with respect and they should treat us with respect as well. The problem is that although many do, there are quite a few who don't. *Almost all accidents involving cars and bikes are the fault of the motorists*. Regardless of where the fault lies, when bikes and cars collide, the bottom line is the cyclist always gets the worst of it. Part of the problem is visibility. In a road filled with cars and trucks, a cyclist can almost become invisible. That invisibility, along with the fact that many motorists are distracted by cell phones and texting, spells trouble! Cyclists should go out of their way to make themselves visible as well as clearly signal motorists of their every intention. As a cyclist, you should always yield to an unresponsive or irritated motorist! The responsibility to avoid dangerous situations ultimately lies with the cyclist. Below is a list of ways in which cyclists can make it safer for everyone.

- Wear bright colored clothing with reflective strips
- Use both a handle bar light and a seat post light when conditions warrant
- Always signal your intentions with good, clear signals
- Avoid rush hour traffic if at all possible
- Avoid using routes that have a high volume of traffic
- Pre-ride routes in an automobile to familiarize yourself with trouble areas
- Be courteous, never allow your emotions to get the best of you
- Report motorists who willingly harass cyclists to the proper authorities
- Never be afraid to get off the bike and walk

WHAT'S LAW AND WHAT'S NOT?

With few exceptions, bicyclists on public roadways assume the same rights and responsibilities as automobile drivers, and are subject to the same state laws and local ordinances. Bicycle laws vary from state to state and for that matter, from city to city. For example, the use of a helmet is required in some cities and not in others.

TEXAS BICYCLE LAWS

These "rules of the road" are based on Texas Transportation Code statutes. Laws are designed to improve the safety of everyone who uses the roadways. Don't become a statistic! Remember to always use hand signals and body actions to communicate with motorists and other bicyclists.

Bicyclists have the rights and duties of other vehicle operators: (551.101)

Yes, this means you have to stop at stop signs and red lights, but cars are required to yield right-of-way to a bicycle when appropriate, just as to any other vehicle.

Ride near the curb and go in the same direction as other traffic: (551.103)

Near the curb is subjective (we recommend leaving a cushion of about three feet) but the law gives a cyclist the right to take the lane when necessary for safety.

At least one hand on the handlebars (two are safer): (551.102c)

One when signaling but two when turning, works well.

Use hand and arm signals: (545.107)

Point the way you are going, let the other operators know what you want to do.

One rider per saddle: (551.102a)

Don't let your friends share your bike while riding unless you're both on a tandem.

You may ride two abreast as long as you don't impede traffic: (551.103c)

Racing and taking the lane are special cases.

Must have a white light on the front and a red reflector or red light on the rear (for riding at night): (551.104b)

The light is primarily so people can see you coming from the side, where their headlights do not shine on your reflectors. The law, effective as of Sept. 2001, states that a red light can replace a red reflector.

Brakes capable of making the braked wheel skid: (551.104a)

Don't test that front brake to see if the wheel will skid while riding, especially downhill.

Texas Transportation Code

Sec. 545.107. Method of Giving Hand and Arm Signals

An operator who is permitted to give a hand and arm signal shall give the signal from the left side of the vehicle as follows:

To make a left turn signal, extend hand and arm horizontally;

To make a right turn signal, extend hand and arm upward, except that a bicycle operator may signal from the right side of the vehicle with the hand and arm extended horizontally; and to stop or decrease speed, extend hand and arm downward.

Chapter 551
Operation of Bicycles, Mopeds, and Play Vehicles

SUBCHAPTER A. APPLICATION OF CHAPTER

Sec. 551.001. Persons Affected

This chapter applies only to a person operating a bicycle on:

A highway; or

A path set aside for the exclusive operation of bicycles.

Sec. 551.002. Moped Included

A provision of this subtitle applicable to a bicycle also applies to a moped, other than a provision that by its nature, cannot apply to a moped.

SUBCHAPTER B. REGULATION OF OPERATION

Sec. 551.101. Rights and Duties

(a) A person operating a bicycle has the rights and duties applicable to a driver operating a vehicle under this subtitle, unless:

A provision of this chapter alters a right or duty; or

A right or duty applicable to a driver operating a vehicle cannot by its nature apply to a person operating a bicycle.

(b) A parent of a child or a guardian of a ward may not knowingly permit the child or ward to violate this subtitle.

Sec. 551.102. General Operation

(a) A person operating a bicycle shall ride only on or astride a permanent and regular seat attached to the bicycle.

(b) A person may not use a bicycle to carry more persons than the bicycle is designed or equipped to carry.

(c) A person operating a bicycle may not use the bicycle to carry an object that prevents the person from operating the bicycle with at least one hand on the handlebars of the bicycle.

(d) A person operating a bicycle, coaster, sled, or toy vehicle, or using roller skates may not attach either the person or the bicycle, coaster, sled, toy vehicle, or roller skates to a streetcar or vehicle on a roadway.

551.103. Operation on Roadway

(a) Except as provided by Subsection (b), a person operating a bicycle on a roadway who is moving slower than the other traffic on the roadway shall ride as near as practicable to the right curb or edge of the roadway, unless:

(1) The person is passing another vehicle moving in the same direction;

(2) The person is preparing to turn left at an intersection or onto a private road or driveway;

(3) A condition on or off the roadway, including a fixed or moving object, parked or moving vehicle, pedestrian, animal, or surface hazard prevents the person from safely riding next to the right curb or edge of the roadway; or

(4) The person is operating a bicycle in an outside lane that is:

(A) less than 14 feet in width and does not have a designated bicycle lane adjacent to that lane; or

(B) too narrow for a bicycle and a motor vehicle to safely travel side by side.

(b) A person operating a bicycle on a one-way roadway with two or more marked traffic lanes may ride as near as practicable to the left curb or edge of the roadway.

(c) Persons operating bicycles on a roadway may ride two abreast. Persons riding two abreast on a laned roadway shall ride in a single lane. Persons riding two abreast may not impede the normal and reasonable flow of traffic on the roadway. Persons may not ride more than two abreast unless they are riding on a part of a roadway set aside for the exclusive operation of bicycles.

(d) Repealed by Acts 2001, 77th Leg., ch. 1085, § 13, eff. Sept. 1, 2001.

Acts 1995, 74th Leg., ch. 165, $ 1, eff. Sept. 1, 1995.
Amended by Acts 2001, 77th Leg., ch. 1085, $$ 10, 13, eff. Sept. 1, 2001.

Sec. 551.104. Safety Equipment

(a) A person may not operate a bicycle unless the bicycle is equipped with a brake capable of making a braked wheel skid on dry, level, clean pavement.

(b) A person may not operate a bicycle at night-time unless the bicycle is equipped with:

(1) A lamp on the front of the bicycle that emits a white light visible from a distance of a least 500 feet in front of the bicycle; and

(2) On the rear of the bicycle:

(A) a red reflector that is:

(i) of a type approved by the department; and

(ii) visible when directly in front of lawful upper beams of motor vehicle headlamps from all distances from 50 to 300 feet to the rear of the bicycle; or

(B) lamp that emits a red light visible from a distance of 500 feet to the rear of the bicycle.

(C) In addition to the reflector required by Subsection (b), a person operating a bicycle at night-time may use a lamp on the rear of the bicycle that emits a red light visible from a distance of 500 feet to the rear of the bicycle.

Sec. 551.105. Competitive Racing

(a) In this section, "bicycle" means a non-motorized vehicle propelled by human power.

(b) A sponsoring organization may hold a competitive bicycle race on a public road only with the approval of the appropriate local law enforcement agencies.

(c) The local law enforcement agencies and the sponsoring organization may agree on safety regulations governing the movement of bicycles during a competitive race or during training for a competitive race, including the permission for bicycle operators to ride abreast.

PROPER ETIQUETTE

Etiquette is basically unwritten laws that cyclists should follow. It's the ole "do unto others as you would have them do unto you." Listening to headphones, talking on the phone, or texting while riding, are just a few examples of poor etiquette, not to mention quite dangerous. While distracted, cyclists inadvertently hold up traffic, swerve in and out of lanes, and are simply unaware of what's happening around them. This type of behavior usually makes the relationship between motorists and cyclists even unhealthier than it already is. While it's true that the same can be said for motorists, we as cyclists must set an example if we wish to make cycling safer for all.

RIDING IN A GROUP

I encourage everyone to find a group to ride with, you will truly enjoy it. Although riding in a group is a lot of fun, for beginners it can be somewhat overwhelming. This is normally because beginners aren't sure what they are supposed to do or not do. The truth is, many experienced riders could learn a thing or two from this section. For group rides to be safe, everyone has to be on the same page. My good friend Dennis Smith took the time to put together a simple set of rules and etiquette that should give you the confidence necessary to be a bit more relaxed, thus making the experience much safer and certainly more enjoyable.

Think you want to go on a group road ride? There is a lot going on in a group that may not be evident to the uninitiated rider. Some of the roadies and I have come up with a list of etiquette rules that generally make for a safer and more cohesive ride. Interested in learning? Read on.

- There is no "I" in group. If every rider in the group will show more concern for the safety of his fellow riders than himself, everyone will get home safely and have a good ride.
- Ride 2 by 2. Don't ride 3-wide across the road. Where does the rider in the middle go to escape trouble?
- When the group approaches a stop sign or light, stay behind the rider in front of you. Don't bunch up. When you start up again, if a rider misses a clip-in, you could touch wheels and someone will fall.

- Don't overreact to things in or on the road: dogs, holes, etc. Your quick and unexpected movement may take someone down. Look ahead through the group and stay alert. Make subtle changes of your line and make sure your fellow riders are aware of your intentions. Make sure you have room to do the move.
- Signal road hazards by pointing at them. Don't loose control by taking a hand off the bars if there isn't time to signal before you get in the hazard.
- Don't hesitate to say, "right turn," "left turn," "car up," or "car back." You don't need to scream and scare the daylights out of everyone. Just say it loud enough to be heard.
- If you want to talk, fine, but don't turn and look at the listener. Keep your eyes ahead.
- If you have a flat or mechanical problem, don't slam on the brakes in the middle of the group. Call out your problem and when it's clear to the back and side, move to the edge of the road. Just let your fellow riders know what is going on.
- Feeling strong? Work on the front, not off of it. Put your effort into giving your fellow riders a draft to follow. If you ride 20 yards in front of the group at the same speed the group is going, someone else still has to work at the front. It's wasted energy that you or someone else may need later in the ride.
- On a climb that you want to put a big effort into, go ahead. When you get to the top, sit up and let the group come back to you. Don't make them chase while you dangle just in front.
- When the group is on a climb and very close, remember to leave at least a wheel length between you and the bike in front of you. If the rider in front of you goes to stand on the pedals, unless he makes a conscious effort to pull the bike up under him, it will move rearward, putting his rear wheel into your front and you will fall down.
- Overlapping Wheels: Simply put, NEVER do it! When your front wheel is hit by a rear wheel, you will fall down. If you don't fall, apply for sainthood because a miracle has just happened.
- When you and a fellow rider are at the front of the group making a pull and your turn is up, the rider on the right goes back on the right side and the rider on the left goes back on the left. ALWAYS. Never cross in front of the group. If the road is narrow, let either the right or left riders go back one at a time.
- If there are an odd number of riders when the lead changes and the riders coming off get to the rear; if you are the odd rider at the back, either be behind the right or left hand rider, not in the middle.
- When you are not in the back, keep your hands on the bars. Eat, drink, stretch, or whatever when there is no one behind you.
- When you are in the lead, watch where you are going. The safety of the whole group depends on you. It's hard to see ahead looking at your crank arms.
- When it's your turn to take the lead, don't immediately jump the speed up. Hold it at what the group has been traveling. The riders that just got off may not be able to make the higher pace after their effort. Give them a chance to catch their breath. Gradually raise the speed. It's not a race.

- Don't do more than you can. It doesn't gain anything putting all your effort into one hill or one pull and then getting dropped. Most strong riders just need a little break. Don't try to equal their work. Do the best you can. That's all any rider expects.

http://www.youtube.com/watch?v=rsZKysNJZnc

- Going through corners, stay behind the rider in front of you. Don't cut inside of everyone. The group is setting up for the turn based on what they see. If you suddenly appear in the middle of the turn, it makes for some hairy moves if you cut in front of everyone.

RULES OF THE ROAD CHAPTER TEST

1. List 2 examples of poor etiquette while cycling. _____
   _____
   _____

2. Name 3 hand signals that cyclists must use while riding. _____
   _____
   _____

3. Cyclists should go out of their way to make themselves _____ as well
   as clearly signal motorists of their every intention.

4. What 2 pieces of equipment do you need, on your bike, in order to ride at night? _____
   _____
   _____

5. The responsibility to avoid dangerous situations ultimately lies with the cyclist. List at
   least 3 ways in which cyclists can make it safer for everyone. _____
   _____
   _____
   _____
   _____

6. A bicyclist under the Texas Vehicle Code:
   a. always has the right of way
   b. has the same rights and responsibilities as divers of vehicles
   c. must always yield to other vehicles

CHAPTER 9

Riding Fundamentals

GETTING ON AND OFF YOUR BIKE

Believe it or not, there is actually a right as well as a wrong way to get on and off your bike. To get on your bike, stand to one side of the bike and place both hands on the handlebars. Next tilt the bike toward you and swing the leg closest to the bike over the seat, placing the foot on the ground so that you are straddling the top tube.

Always make sure you come to a complete stop before trying to get off your bike. Once you have come to a stop put both feet on the ground. Next step away from the bike with your dominant leg and tilt the bike toward that leg. Finally, holding the handlebars with both hands, swing the leg closest to the bike over the seat placing the foot on the ground. That's it, you're off!

STARTING

Once you have climbed aboard your bike and are ready to go, there are a couple of important fundamentals you'll need to apply. First and foremost, remember when you only have two wheels, you need momentum to stay upright. Once you lose momentum, one of two things will happen—you will either have to put your foot on the ground to hold yourself and the bike up or you, as well as the bike, will fall! Since you're sitting still, you have no momentum and will need to generate some. Place the pedal that corresponds to your dominant leg a quarter of the way past the top of the power stroke. With both hands on the handle bars, push the pedal forward with a good amount of force. At the same time, sit on the seat and raise your other foot and place it on the opposite pedal.

STOPPING

Stopping requires a few important fundamentals as well. Most important, familiarize yourself with the front and back brakes. The brake lever on the left controls the front wheel while the brake lever on the right controls the back wheel. Generally speaking, most of the stopping is done by applying the back brakes and then just feathering the front brakes until the bike has come to a stop. Too much front brake can send you over the handlebars in what

© spfotocz, 2012. Used under license from Shutterstock, Inc.

is commonly called an **endo**, which by the way, can be quite painful. Be very aware when resting your hands on the brake levers when riding. A simple bad spot in the road such as a bump or a pothole can cause you to tighten your grip to gain control of the bike and in doing so, you could apply too much brake causing you to fall. Brakes are used more frequently when mountain biking and thus requires one to have the hands placed on the levers a good deal of the time. It is a really good idea to simply put two fingers on the rear brake lever and only one on the front lever. Since mountain bike terrain is much rougher than the road, it becomes much easier to lock down the brakes by accident. The one finger will be less apt to take control as opposed to the two fingers on the back.

STEERING

Most people think that steering a bike means simply turning the handlebars. The truth is, about the only time you just turn the handlebars to steer is when you're at low speeds navigating an area such as a parking lot. Steering a bike through turns requires little or no movement with the handlebars at all. The direction in which the bike

goes is controlled by the placement of weight. First look where you want the bike to go, pick a line to follow through the turn. Then simply put the foot opposite of the direction you're turning to the bottom of the pedal stroke causing the inside foot to be up. Next, feel your weight on the saddle, push directly down through the seat post into the bottom bracket and finally push forward a little on the inside hand while pushing down on the outside pedal. This will cause the bike to lean into the turn and follow your line. Remember, going down a hill causes your weight to lean a little forward so try to keep your weight toward the back of the saddle.

Hand placement is also important when steering a bike. Generally speaking, cornering should be done with the hands on the hoods or the drops but not on the tops. Both the drops and the hoods allow you to easily access the brakes, the drops however, are better for higher speeds because they lower your center of gravity.

http://www.youtube.com/watch?v=um6N2LK7BQA

CHANGING GEARS

Changing gears is an important part of riding a bike. Learning to change gears properly can make riding much more fun. When you change gears you are effectively changing the size of your wheels, without actually changing your wheels. Why is it important to be able to do this, you might ask; well, here is the answer. A small wheel is really easy to pedal and great for steep hills but will not take you anywhere in a hurry. A big wheel is much harder to pedal and can get you

where you want to go a lot quicker, great for long flat straight-a-ways! Since roads have both hills and flat areas, we need both big and little wheels!

What you need to remember is really quite simple. We can change the size of our wheels by simply changing gears. The shifter on the left controls the front derailleur that moves the chain from one chain ring to another. The shifter on the right controls the rear derailleur that moves the chain from one cog (rings connected to the back hub) to another. A combination of the largest chain ring in the front and the smallest cog in the back puts the bike in the highest gear, which requires the most effort to pedal (our big wheel); while a combo of the smallest chain ring in the front and the largest cog in the back puts the bike in the lowest gear, which requires the least amount of effort to pedal (our little wheel).

The number of gears you have at your disposal is found by multiplying the front rings and the back cogs together. For example, if the front of your bike has 3 chain rings and the back has a cassette that consists of 7 cogs, then you would have 21 gears (3 x 7). Several gears overlap and are really of little use. The combinations though are quite useful in allowing us to keep our efforts at a minimum regardless of road elevation changes. Some combinations, however, should be avoided: such as the big chain ring in the front combined with the big cog in the back or the small chain ring in the front combined with the small cog in the back. These combinations often are referred to as **cross chaining** and can result in the chain being dropped from the rings altogether as well as unnecessary wear and tear on the ring, cog teeth, and chain.

http://www.youtube.com/watch?v=V1sV_JPHnoY

CADENCE / SPINNING

There is definitely more than meets the eye when it comes to pedaling a bicycle. The simplest way to explain how to properly pedal is by introducing a term known as **cadence**. Cadence refers to the number of revolutions per minute that the pedals rotate. The most efficient number of rotations for the average person is 80-100 rpm.

To maintain the desired cadence, it is important to select the proper gear. If you choose a gear that causes your cadence to be greater than 100 rpm, it will cause you to wobble and bounce up and down on your saddle. If you choose a gear that causes your cadence to be lower than 80 rpm, it will force your legs to work hard and cause a buildup of lactic acid, resulting in pain. The best approach to learning to maintain a cadence is to find a flat stretch of road and practice. Then move to a road that has a few slight elevation changes and use your gears to keep the legs moving the same. As you move up the hills, lowering your gears will allow your cadence to remain the same. When going down a hill, change to a higher gear to maintain proper cadence. Remember, however, that the higher gear going up hills makes maintaining the cadence easier but also decreases the speed at which you will move up the hill, just as the lower gear going down the hill will cause you to gain speed. It is best when going down steep hills to sometimes stop pedaling until the decent is over and you are back on a level stretch of road.

http://www.youtube.com/watch?v=KOhzk4jv7wQ

ROAD OBSTACLES

Learning to navigate around road obstacles is a must if you're going to ride a bike. When we use the term *road obstacles*, the first thing that comes to mind are things that are lying in the road such as bottles or cans, boxes, animal carcasses, physical things, etc. There are other obstacles that are even more dangerous because the inexperienced bicyclist doesn't necessarily notice them. For example, road cracks, gravel, pot holes, and even road stripes are far more dangerous than a physical object lying in the road. Only a small portion of a road bike tire actually touches the road, so a patch of gravel or a wet road stripe can

© iStockphoto/Thinkstock

cause a tire to lose its grip on the surface thus causing a rider to lose control and fall.

The best way to deal with road obstacles is to avoid them by steering around them. Although that sounds easy enough, it actually requires the rider's full attention the entire time they are on the bike. Looking down for just a second can cause you to hit a crack that hadn't come into view yet. If you're on a road with a very small shoulder or no shoulder at all, avoiding obstacles may cause you to have to move into traffic. To ride a bike safely, you must be fully aware of your surroundings at all times. That

means understanding what to look for in road conditions, being aware of traffic patterns, and staying alert at all times. And NO headphones!

Sometimes you may have to simply stop and lift your bike over obstructions. More advanced riders can perform a skill known as **bunny hopping** to jump their bike over the obstacle. This is a great skill to possess but should not be attempted until you have perfected it in a safe place, such as a playground or park.

http://www.youtube.com/watch?v=d2T5dfOHcbQ

RIDING FUNDAMENTALS CHAPTER TEST

1. In order to ride a bike safely, you must be fully aware of your _____ at all times.

2. What is the first thing a person needs to do before attempting to get off a bike? _____
   _____

3. Hand placement is also important when steering a bike. Cornering should be done with the hands on the hoods or the drops, but not on the tops.
   True or False?

4. Starting – Put the following steps in the correct order.

   _____ Sit on the seat and raise your other foot and place it on the opposite pedal.
   _____ Place the pedal that corresponds to your dominant leg one quarter of the way past the top of the power stroke.
   _____ With both hands on the handlebars, push the pedal forward with a good amount of force.

5. When is about the only time you turn the handlebars to steer your bike? _____
   _____

6. Too much front brake can send you over the handlebars in what is commonly referred to as _____.

7. The brake lever on the left controls the _____ wheel while the brake lever on the right controls the _____ wheel.

8. When getting on your bike, your hands should be placed where? _____
   _____

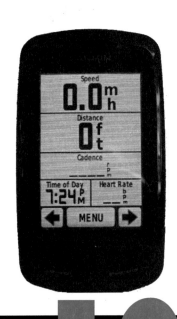

CHAPTER 10

Planning a Ride

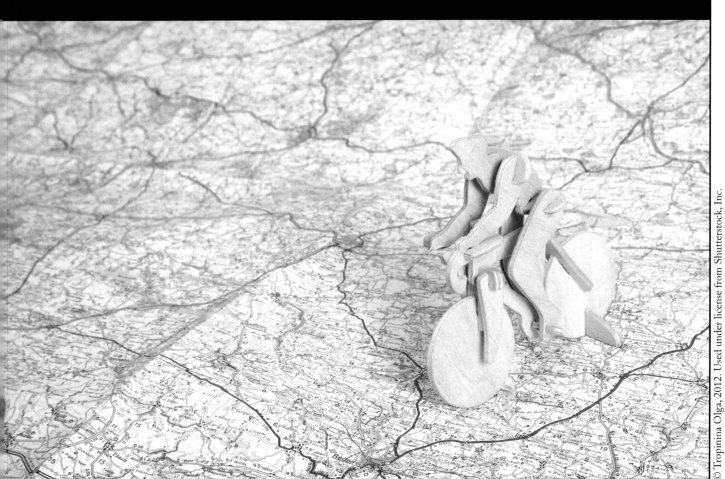

PRE-RIDING A ROUTE

A little preparation goes a long way in ensuring that your upcoming ride is not only enjoyable, but safe. In general, the less surprises, the better. The best way to familiarize yourself with a planned route is to pre-ride the route in an automobile. Being familiar with a route doesn't necessarily mean you've driven the route several times and know your way. For example, if you have decided that you're going to ride your bike to work or to a friend's house, you will probably be familiar with the area and possible problems on the way (for a car) but what about for a bike? Bikes don't travel the same speed as cars, they are far more affected by weather and road conditions than are cars, and they are certainly not as protecting when it comes to unforeseen obstacles as are cars! Before you make the ride on your bike, you should make the trip in a car again and imagine you're on a bike. Make note of things that will be beneficial to making your ride enjoyable and safe. Below are a few things to consider on your pre-ride.

TRAFFIC – Traffic plays a huge role in helping us determine the best and safest route. Remember, bicyclists are easily overlooked when in heavy traffic. Extremely busy intersections become much more dangerous on a bike and if possible, should be avoided.

ROAD CONDITIONS – The type of road surface greatly affects not only the speed at which you can travel but the amount of energy you will have to expend to move the bike forward. Deformities in the road, such as cracks or pot holes, are much more dangerous for a bike than for an automobile and must be taken into consideration.

ELEVATION CHANGES – An automobile can make short work of a hill whereas a short hill can make a bicyclist rethink his or her desire to ride a bike! A hill that is barely noticeable in a car can be quite a challenge for a cyclist. A route that has less abrupt elevation changes, even though it may be longer, might be a better choice for the average cyclist.

TIME OF DAY – The length of your route in an automobile and on a bike might be very similar but the time it takes to cover that distance could vary greatly. Just because you miss rush hour by 20 minutes when driving your automobile doesn't mean you will when riding your bike. Your automobile may also get you to your destination before darkness with time to spare, your bicycle may not. Riding a bike in rush hour or after dark is dangerous and should be avoided, if possible. Make sure you consider the route in terms of bicycle time.

LENGTH OF RIDE – Riding a bike is the most efficient means of transportation and actually requires less effort than walking. That being said, the length of time on a bicycle, however, can still be more taxing than one thinks. Being on a bike for an extended period of time, for example, can cause your back, hands, feet, and rear-end to experience discomfort. This discomfort causes tension and thus can lead to a less than enjoyable experience. Know your limitations and your comfort zone. The more you ride, the longer you will be able to ride comfortably and safely.

OBSTACLES ALONG THE WAY – There are many obstacles that go virtually unnoticed when in an automobile but are of great concern when on a bicycle. The first that comes to mind is dogs. Although dogs are usually just playing around when they are biting at your ankles or wheels, the consequences can be quite devastating. Routes that take you through neighborhoods where dogs run freely should be avoided, if possible. Areas that are high in crime rate that you can zip through in an automobile aren't so easily managed on a bike and should be avoided as well.

The above areas, by no means, cover everything that should be considered before setting out on a ride. Hopefully, however, they will provide you with the proper mindset for planning a ride. The better thought-out the ride, the more enjoyable and safe it will be!

RIDING APPLICATIONS

Riding apps such as *Map My Ride* are very useful when planning a ride. These programs allow you to lay out a route and will provide you with valuable info such as elevation changes, distances, approximate ride time, and so forth. The route can also be uploaded to your GPS device so that you can be sure to stay on course. Most apps have a lite version that is free as well as a version that is much more comprehensive for a fee. Other apps include: Bikely.com, Gmap-pedometer.com, Veloroutes.org, and Routeslip.com.

INFORM FAMILY OR FRIENDS OF YOUR RIDE

It's always a good idea to let family or friends know when you are going on a ride, especially a long one, not only for your sake but for theirs. If there is an emergency, they will know where to find you or at least where to start looking. Just some basic information can be quite helpful.

WHEN YOU LEAVE – Inform family or friends of the time you are leaving.

YOUR ROUTE – Provide information about your route, this can be easily done with the above-mentioned riding app. You can send a copy of your exact route via email to your family or friends.

WHEN YOU RETURN – Once you return, let someone know you have made it safely.

Bicycling can be such an enjoyable pastime but it can also be dangerous. Following the advice in this chapter will go a long way in making it a much safer and more enjoyable experience.

Last but not least, all cyclists should wear a Road ID when riding their bike. A Road ID is simply a bracelet or necklace that can provide valuable information to someone who's trying to help you if you are in an accident. It has information such as your name, contacts in case of an emergency, and any medical info that is important like medicine allergies. This info should be carried on a cyclist at all times and Road ID is a great way to do it.

http://www.youtube.com/watch?v=Ujvz826mqNY

PLANNING A RIDE CHAPTER TEST

1. The best way to familiarize yourself with a planned route is to _____ the route in an automobile.

2. List 6 things that you should consider on your pre-ride: _____
   _____
   _____
   _____
   _____
   _____

3. How can a riding app such as *Map My Ride* help you plan your ride? _____
   _____
   _____
   _____

4. What 3 things should you inform your family or friends of before your ride? _____
   _____
   _____
   _____

5. How can wearing a Road ID help you if you are in a cycling accident? _____
   _____
   _____
   _____

CHAPTER 11

Fitness and Nutrition

IMPORTANCE OF FITNESS

Today's sedentary lifestyle can lead to cardiovascular disease, stroke, diabetes, and obesity. It also affects energy levels, sleep patterns, and mental wellness. Physical fitness is an effective way of avoiding the above health problems and can be one of the most important things in life and one of the most valuable assets one can ever have. ***Good health can lead to a happy and well-balanced life***. Being physically fit can have many advantages, below are just a few.

CARDIOVASCULAR ENDURANCE: Cardiovascular endurance is the measurement of your heart's strength. It also implies the ability of the body to deliver oxygen and nutrients to tissues and to remove wastes. Physical fitness helps you achieve cardiovascular endurance and helps to increase the oxygen flow to all the body muscles.

MUSCULAR STRENGTH: A balanced and regular fitness regimen helps to increase the ability of muscles to exert force and sustain contraction. In short, a regular workout will make your muscles stronger and thus, increase your overall strength.

SELF-CONFIDENCE: When you look good and you feel good, it is obvious that you have no inhibitions and insecurities to bog you down. A healthy mind and a healthy body are a big boost to your self-confidence!

FLEXIBILITY: Regular exercise will ensure that you move your joints and muscles to their fullest extent and it will increase the flexibility of these joints and your overall body. Flexibility in body movements is achieved only through physical fitness.

BODY COMPOSITION: One of the indicators of physical fitness is a balanced and healthy body composition. Minimum of fat and maximum of lean mass is a sign of a healthy and fit body. The lean mass includes muscles, bones, vital tissues, and organs.

BEAUTIFUL YOU! Exercise and overall fitness helps you detoxify your body and thus, lets your skin breathe. It also helps to tone your body and thus, enhances your overall appearance. In short, physical fitness keeps you beautiful and glowing!

HEALTHY MIND: A healthy mind dwells in a healthy body. Any exercise included in your fitness regimen, will lead to the production of endorphins in the body. Endorphins are chemicals that make you feel happy and a healthy, physically fit body is almost always accompanied by a healthy mind.

DRIVE-AWAY ILLNESS: Moderated and balanced workout in a fitness regimen helps boost the immune system of the body. Fully functional and strong body immunity means that your body develops the strength to ward off diseases and infections.

It's easy to see the benefits but finding the time in our busy schedules is tough. Most means of getting in better shape have us joining gyms, taking classes, or driving our family crazy while we grunt to some new exercise video. All these activities can have positive results but require time that many of us just don't have; which brings us to bicycling.

Bicycling, as a regular aerobic exercise, tends to lead to a healthy body, helps prevent disease and a shortened lifespan, and has several advantages over other exercises:

- First and foremost, bicycling is exciting and fun!
- Little or no time has to be lost, as bike travel can be used to get to work, perform errands, or just enjoy the outdoors.
- One can ride a bicycle almost anywhere, at any time of the year, and cycling is not only inexpensive but it can actually save you money.
- Cycling exercises the heart better than walking without the pounding of jogging and over all, is easier on the body than other forms of exercise.
- Commuting by bike reduces pollution that causes asthma and bronchitis.

So, in short, to have a sense of satisfaction in your life—it is not just the materialistic things that you need—it is your own physical fitness, which will help you in the long run. A disease-free, healthy body and mind are simply priceless! **Riding a bike is one of the simplest, easiest ways to exercise and certainly one of the most enjoyable**. So live life to the fullest, but more important, live wisely and invest time in your own health. *Get on your bike and Ride!!!!*

For those who struggle to find daylight to bike during the week or live in areas where the winter months can be harsh, give a Spin class a try. Spin classes are a great way to meet new people, have fun, and most of all, they help keep you physically fit.

FUELING THE BODY

First and foremost, eating healthily is a part of ones' overall fitness and is something everyone should do, regardless of their level of physical activity. When participating in a physically-challenging sport, nutrition plays a huge role in our ability to perform well. What we eat basically serves as the fuel for our engines. The type of fuel necessary to perform well differs greatly depending on the type and length of the physical activity. What we eat, when we eat, and how much we eat will depend on where we are in the activity. **It is very important that we take in the proper fuel before, during, and after a long ride or race**.

Before

- Three or four days before a long ride or a race you should begin to really hydrate your body. You want to make sure you are drinking plenty of water this whole time. Don't overdo it, but consume enough water so that your urine is light in color or even clear. The single, biggest factor that could hinder your performance is being dehydrated. **Losing as little as 1% of your body weight in fluid can reduce your performance by as much as 10%!** Try to take in 1/2 to 1 ounce of fluid per pound of body weight every day (primarily water).

- Many sources say you should eat a big carbohydrate meal the night before a long ride or race. Doing so tends to leave you feeling bloated, so a better idea is to eat a big carbohydrate meal two nights before a ride or race. The night before the race, eat a light "carb" meal such as pasta, brown rice, a green vegetable, fish or chicken. Don't overdo it; eat until you are just about full. Your body will actually be full at that point. You basically want a meal that is easily digested. This meal should be finished a minimum of 12 hours before the ride or race.

- It is very important that you eat a good breakfast the morning of the ride or race. Make sure you are completely finished at least 2 to 3 hours before your start time. You want the meal to be digested and leave your stomach by ride or race time. As far as what to eat, some athletes have a blended liquid breakfast. They feel this helps in the need to hydrate and digests faster. Others will eat foods high in carbohydrates like oatmeal, whole grain bread toast with peanut butter, bagels, and waffles. Stay away from protein foods like meat or eggs—they tend to digest slowly. Also, no white bread or sugared cereal—the sugar will give you a quick boost of energy and then you will fall off just as fast.
- If you get hungry before the race, have a quick energy bar. Be sure to keep drinking water or a sports drink with electrolytes in small amounts all the way up to start time.

The No. 1 rule of pre-race nutrition is to never try something new on race day. Whatever you choose for your meal, it should be something you have eaten pre-ride before and had no unfavorable reaction. No matter how safe a food seems, you never know how you'll react under stress. Avoid high-fiber carbohydrates, because they can cause cramping when you're hunched over your handlebars, and stay away from caffeine, a diuretic. Some athletes swear by a pre-race energy drink, but any boost you get from the caffeine and sugar will be more than mitigated by the fluid loss caused by the diuretic during the race.

During

According to Lance Armstrong, the following is a good rule of thumb for staying fueled during a ride.

- *Chow Down Early* – Start eating in the first couple hours then eat something every hour after that. Avoid high-fat, high-protein energy bars. Exercising requires carbohydrates, which should be the first ingredient listed on the label. The key is to eat before you feel hungry.
- *Drink Early and Often* – The typical person loses up to 96 ounces daily from sweating, urinating, and exhaling. Extremely hot weather can double or even triple that amount. Drink 3-4 ounces every 10 minutes during a ride. Always carry 2 full water bottles on your frame.
- *Grab a Sandwich* – Make a sandwich of turkey and cheese, or use ingredients of your preference. Cut the sandwich into 4 pieces and wrap them in foil. The pieces should fit easily into your jersey pockets.
- *Munch on Fruit and Bars* – Bananas and energy bars are also good to eat, and easy to peel or unwrap while pedaling.
- *Eat on Downhills or Flats* – The extra effort will interfere with chewing your food.

Continue drinking every 15 minutes and eating every 30 minutes for the duration of the ride.

After

The two most important components of recovery are:

- Replenishing the glycogen fuel burned during the workout
- Rebuilding the muscle proteins that are destroyed

Basically this means replenishing our carbohydrates and proteins lost during the activity.

Most athletes consume too much protein and not enough carbohydrates. Generally speaking, a person can consume about 1 gram of protein for every 10 pounds of body weight and about 4 times that in carbohydrates within an hour or so after completing an intense workout.

The optimal formula for post-exercise nutritional recovery should be approximately 4 grams of carbohydrates for every 1 gram of protein. The 4:1 ratio of carbohydrates to protein maximizes insulin release and maximizes the rate of glycogen/protein synthesis. A recovery drink should be taken in within 30 minutes of the completion of the activity for maximum results.

A 16-ounce bottle of (1%) chocolate milk can basically serve as the perfect recovery drink for a person who weighs between 150-170 pounds.

Electrolyte replenishment is also crucial in the recovery process. Electrolytes can be replaced by consuming fruits, vegetables, and sports drinks. Electrolyte replacement should be done throughout the activity.

1 cup vanilla yogurt + 1 cup fresh fruit (60 grams carbs)
Bonus Benefit: provides over 40% of your daily calcium needs

1 cup orange juice + 1 banana (52 grams carbs)
Bonus Benefit: packs almost 200% of the Daily Value for vitamin C

1 slice banana nut bread + 1 cup skim milk (about 45 grams carbs)
Bonus Benefit: gives you 25% of the Daily Value for calcium

1 PowerBar energy bar + 8 oz PowerBar Endurance sports drink (62 grams carbs)
Bonus Benefit: provides plenty of sodium and potassium to keep you well hydrated

Smoothie of 2 cups skim or soy milk + 1-1/2 cups strawberries + 2 Tbsp soy protein (about 50 grams carbs)
Bonus Benefit: contributes about 5 grams of fiber

1-1/2 cups multigrain cereal + 1-1/2 cups skim milk (54 grams carbs)
Bonus Benefit: contains over 100% of the Daily Value for iron

1 bagel + 1 banana + 1 Tbsp nut butter (about 75 grams carbs)
Bonus Benefit: provides 12 grams of protein

TEN SIMPLE THINGS TO REMEMBER FOR OPTIMAL NUTRITION

1. **Come back to Earth** - Choose the least-processed foods, specifically carbohydrates, when building the majority of your meals
2. **Eat a rainbow often** - Eat a variety of fruits and vegetables in a multitude of color
3. **The fewer legs the better** - The fewer legs the animal has before you consume it, the better the source
4. **Eat fats that give something back** - Raw nuts, seeds, olive oil, nut butters, and omega-3 fatty acids
5. **Three for Three** - 3 main nutrients (carbohydrates, protein, and fat) every 3 hours
6. **Eat breakfast every day** - Eating breakfast will give the body the fuel it needs, jumpstart the metabolism, and set people up to consume the number of calories they should take in each day
7. **Hydrate** - 1/2 to 1 ounce of fluid per pound of body weight every day (primarily water)
8. **Don't waste your workout** - Always consume a post workout recovery drink within 30 minutes after completion of the activity
9. **Supplement wisely** - Supplements should only complement the diet
10. **Get back into the kitchen** - The more you prepare your own food, the more control you will have in the nourishment of your body

If it doesn't spoil quickly, you probably shouldn't eat it!

Remember that the concept of eating more carbohydrates during your heaviest training is more important than trying to adhere to specific numbers. But when you're upping the miles on your rides, adding just one of these mini meals per day gives you the extra carbohydrates you need to keep riding strong.

CROSS-TRAINING

For those of you who really enjoy cycling and wish to improve your overall cycling fitness, cross-training is a must. Cross-training in sports and fitness refers to the combining of exercises to work various parts of the body. Often, one particular activity works certain muscle groups and areas of fitness much more than others; cross-training aims to eliminate this. When it comes to cycling, all muscle groups are worked, however, some are certainly worked harder.

Many believe cross-training is something cyclists should do in the off season. We believe cross-training should be a regular part of your exercise regime year round. When cross-training, a cyclist's goal should be to:

- *Improve the Strength of the Cycling Muscles* – Stationary trainers that offer resistance are a good way of strengthening cycling muscle groups. Weight lifting to isolate certain muscle groups, thus enhancing the strength of the rider, particularly on hills, is beneficial. Doing high-repetition exercises in the gym to train your muscles to fire faster can improve your cycling speed.
- *Improve Aerobic Power* – It's important to train aerobically to maintain your base power. Swimming is an excellent choice, as is running—but be sure to build mileage slowly to prevent injuries. Watch that your heart rate doesn't spike into the anaerobic zone for more than 1 minute at a time—you should be able to continue a conversation while you're exercising.
- *Improve Overall Strength and Flexibility* – Rebalance your body by strengthening your core muscle groups, which aren't as developed by cycling but are essential to generating power on a bike. Yoga or Pilates will work these areas, especially your lower back and stomach. Also, stretch after your rides and cross-training workouts, concentrating on your calves, IT bands, and hamstrings.

FITNESS AND NUTRITION CHAPTER TEST

1. List 3 advantages of being physically fit. _____
   _____
   _____

2. It is very important that we take in the proper fuel _____,
   _____, and _____ a long ride or race.

3. Riding a bike is one of the simplest, easiest ways to exercise.   True or False

4. Losing as little as 1% of your body weight in fluid can reduce your performance by as
   much as _____%

5. The 2 most important components of recovery are _____
   _____

6. How many days before a race should you begin to hydrate? _____

7. You should continue drinking every _____ minutes and eating every___ minutes for the
   duration of the ride.

8. List 2 advantages of bicycling as a form of exercise. _____
   _____

9. The optimal formula for post-exercise nutritional recovery is _____ grams of
   carbohydrates for every _____ gram of protein.

10. List the 3 benefits of cross-training. _____
    _____

CHAPTER 12

Local Bicycle Shops and Clubs

LOCAL BICYCLE SHOPS

I cannot begin to explain how important developing a relationship with a local bike shop in your area is. When I decided to get a bike, the first thing I did was get on the Internet. There is a wealth of information on the Internet and within a few hours I knew everything there was to know about cycling, I was basically an expert! So I picked out a bike and some gear that I felt was right for me and called the local bike shop to get some prices. Their prices were higher than those I had seen online, so I found what I wanted online and ordered it. I saved a lot of money…I thought.

When my bike came in I had to put it together. That had never crossed my mind but it wasn't really that big of a deal, and within about an hour and a half I had a fully functioning bike. The only real problem was that the chain made a lot of noise regardless of what gear I put it in. At first I thought that was normal, but after a few rides with friends I realized something wasn't quite right. Also, I could not believe how much my shoulders and knees hurt after riding. Maybe I was in worse shape than I thought.

I decided to take the bike into the local shop since I couldn't take it back to where I bought it; actually I'm not sure where the bike came from other than a store on the Internet. The guys in the shop were quite helpful, the front and the rear derailleur simply needed adjusting. Seems I had also made a few mistakes in choosing the proper shoes, frame size, and helmet. I had purchased a mountain bike helmet and shoes along with a road bike that was too small for me. Again, not really that big of deal, I simply sold the bike as well as the shoes and the helmet for about 20% less than I gave for them. Then I had to pay to ship the bike to its new owner, some guy bought it from me via the Internet…he got a great deal. Well, now I was ready to get what I needed and the experience only cost me about $500 which, by the way, is way more than what I thought I was going to save by purchasing it on the Internet.

The truth is, local businesses have to pay for a store front, utilities, and inventory, not to mention employees. Yes, they charge more than a guy behind a desk at his house, with no costs other than Internet service, having his products shipped straight from the manufacturer to the consumers. But when the customers have a problem, they want it fixed right then and with an Internet business, that's just not going to happen!

As far as that wealth of knowledge that one can find on the Internet, it too, is a bit overrated. Anyone can post anything and almost everyone is an "expert." As a PGA professional and a business owner, I should have known better. I'm not saying that buying from the Internet is totally taboo, just that you should start the process with your local shop and let them help you make good decisions. After all, you will need their help and services a lot if you continue to bike.

My local shop is Bicycles Outback and it's the best shop in the world! Ian, the owner, has always been more than fair with what he charges me; and Jon has taught me more about riding in 6 months than I could have learned on my own in 5 years. Mike and Glenn are great mechanics who have kept my bikes in awesome shape; Emilie not only helped me choose the right accessories, but also partnered with me in a 12-hour mountain bike race. Dennis has my bikes set up so they feel like they were made just for me; and Fred Schmid, who didn't start riding until age 61 yet won several national championships, has inspired and encouraged me beyond words (he is now 79 and still kicks my tail).

It is a great bicycle shop full of very knowledgeable people who have not only helped me get the right equipment, but have fueled my passion for cycling and more than anything else, have become my friends. I encourage you to take the time to get to know the people who work in your local shop. Let them help you from the beginning—build a relationship with them; you will be glad you did and hopefully you, too, will get the opportunity to tell someone how great your local shop is.

BICYCLE CLUBS

A bicycle club is an organization whose mission is to promote the love of cycling. Their mission is to work hard to service the cycling needs of their area by providing communication and fellowship among cyclists; trail development and maintenance for private and governmental land owners; safety education to schools, churches, and other community organizations; and assistance to individual cyclists and cycling-related charitable activities.

Bicycle clubs usually organize rides for every level of rider. This is a great way to meet fellow cyclists whose skill levels are compatible to yours. To find out about clubs in your area, you can search the Internet or…you guessed it, visit your local bicycle shop!

Local Shop services include:

- Bicycle repairs (on site) many times in the same day
- Bicycle Modifications
- Bicycle Fittings
- Bicycle Sales
- Bicycle Accessories
- Bicycle Nutrition

Not only do bicycle shops have on hand all the things you'll need to safely and enjoyably start bicycling, they provide years of experience in helping you to make the right choices. From what type of bicycle to buy to nutritional needs, from bicycle transportation to classes on how to areas such as repairing a flat. They are always only a phone call away. Many times when all factors are figured in you'll find buying locally is much less expensive than the internet. Developing a relationship with your local bike shop will be worth much more than any bike you ever buy!

CHAPTER 13

Competitions

WHY COMPETE?

That's really a pretty good question. Why would someone put themselves through so many hours of training and hard work? I think a better question is, why not? We compete in our daily lives every day.

Healthy competition is at the heart of every winner—in sports and in life. It is not about cutting corners, cheating, or disrespecting your opponents in an attempt to win. A true competitor is determined to work toward improving their skills and life—putting in the long, hard hours needed to break through plateaus and achieve success. But competing goes beyond sports. Competing is about life. One cannot be complacent with their faith, relationships, work, or even their health and expect to achieve great results or even sustain them.

If you don't work on these things you value every day, they regress. If you let them regress enough, eventually you'll lose them.

Too often we shackle ourselves with self inflicted limitations. "I'm too old to do this or that" or "I just don't have the time." I teach at Baylor University with a gentleman who is 90 years old and still teaching and inspiring young people. I have as a golf student a gentleman who is 83 and stills shoots his age on a weekly basis (he plays 5 days a week). And what's really amazing is that I am a competitive mountain biker and get to ride and train with a gentleman, Fred Schmid, who's about to turn 80. He started biking at age 61 and has since won multiple world and national championships, including several state titles this year.

When asked, "Why race?" here is what Fred had to say. "I ask myself that question while waiting on the start line at every race! For me, 'why race' is just an extension of the question, 'Why ride?' First, it's a fun way to get fit; when you're young, you feel immortal. You're never too old to feel good, and each of us would feel better if we did some sort of regular aerobic activity. Second, it's encouraging to see progress. I like racing because it measures my skill against the consistant performance of other riders. In a race, it's the same conditions for everyone, so you have the opportunity to compare your performance to others and can accurately judge if you're getting better. Third, racing encourages you to train. When you know a race is coming up, you are inspired to get out there, even when the weather is poor, you don't feel strong, or you don't have anyone to ride with. Fourth, comradeship. I can honestly say everyone I ride with, I like. Those guys are accomplished people, who value riding, the outdoors, and fitness. We respect each others' efforts regardless of who wins. That's not a sentiment one feels often when thinking about the competition in business. Fifth, my friendship with my wife. Suzanne bought me my first bike when I thought I might be too old to ride a toy (age 61). We use the racing trips as an excuse to camp, see the national parks, visit friends, and spend some wonderful time together in some very beautiful surroundings. Sixth, racing successfully introduces you to top professionals that you may never get another chance to know. Seventh, to give something back. My racing well gets the message out that you can be successful at a physical activity despite advancing in age. Finally, it's just plain fun! To paraphrase Robert Taylor in *The Last Hunt*, 'Racing? Racing is the only way I know I'm alive.'"

To summarize what my friend, Fred, is saying is simple: **there are a lot of reasons to compete and not a lot of reasons not to!** Competition is a healthy part of life. From experience, I can honestly say that it's a great way to learn a lot about yourself that perhaps you don't know. So get out there and give it a try!

TYPES OF COMPETITIONS

Crit or Criterium

A bike race held on a short course (usually less than 5 km), often run on closed-off city center streets. Race length can be determined by a number of laps or total time, in which case the number of remaining laps is calculated as the race progresses. Generally, the event's duration (commonly one hour) is shorter than that of a traditional road race—which can last many hours, sometimes over the course of several days or even weeks, as in a Grand Tour. However, the average speed and intensity are appreciably higher. The winner is the first rider to cross the finish line without having been "lapped."

Road Race

A bicycle racing sport held on roads, using racing bicycles. The term *road racing* is usually applied to events where competing riders start simultaneously (unless riding a handicap event) with the winner being the first to the line at the end of the course. Historically, the most competitive and devoted countries were Belgium, Colombia, Denmark, France, Germany, Italy, Luxembourg, the Netherlands, Spain, and Switzerland, however, as the sport grows in popularity, countries such as Australia, Venezuela, Russia, South Africa, New Zealand, Norway, the United Kingdom, Ireland, Poland, and the United States continue to produce world class cyclists. Road bicycle racing began as an organized sport in 1868. The first world championship was in 1893 and cycling has

© Marc Pagani Photography, 2012. Used under license from Shutterstock, Inc.

been part of the Olympic Games since the modern sequence started in Athens in 1896. Road racing in its modern form originated in the late 19th century. The sport was popular in the western European countries of France, Spain, Belgium, and Italy. Some of Europe's earliest road bicycle races remain among the sport's biggest events. These early races include Liège–Bastogne–Liège (established 1892), Paris–Roubaix (1896), the Tour de France (1903), the Milan – San Remo and Giro di Lombardia (1905), the Giro d'Italia (1909), and the Ronde van Vlaanderen (1913). They have provided a template for other races around the world. While the sport has spread throughout the world, these historic races remain the most prestigious for a cyclist to win.

Time Trials

A road bicycle race in which cyclists race alone against the clock (in French: *contre la montre* – literally "against the watch," in Italian: tappa a *cronometro* "stopwatch stage"). There are also track-based time trials where riders compete in velodromes, and team time trials (TTT). ITT's or individual time trials are also referred to as **"the race of truth,"** as winning depends only on each rider's strength and endurance, and not on help provided by teammates and others riding ahead and creating a slipstream. Starting times are at equal intervals, usually one or two minutes apart. The starting sequence is usually based on the finishing times in preceding races (or preceding stages in the case of a multi-stage race) with the highest ranked cyclist starting last. Starting later gives the racer the advantage of knowing what time they need to beat (and also makes the event more interesting to spectators). Competitors are not permitted to draft (ride in the slipstream) behind each other. Any help between riders is forbidden. The rider with the fastest time is declared the winner.

Mountain Bike Racing

The Union Cycliste Internationale (UCI) recognized the sport of **mountain bike racing** relatively late in 1990, when it sanctioned the world championships in Purgatory, Colorado. The first mountain biking world cup series took place in 1991. Its 9-race circuit covered 2 continents—Europe and North America—and was sponsored by Grundig. In 1992, the Grundig-UCI world cup circuit expanded to 10 races, and remained a trans-Atlantic series. Cross-country racing was the only world cup sport at this time; then in 1993 a 6-event downhill world cup was introduced. In 1996, cross-country mountain biking events were added to the Olympic Games. NORBA refers to the Board of Trustees that represent the sport of mountain bike racing for USA Cycling. There are 3 USA Cycling Mountain Bike National Calendars:

Endurance, Gravity, and Ultra-Endurance. USA Cycling runs the USA Cycling Mountain Bike National Championships. In 2006, cross-country mountain biking events became part of the World Deaf Cycling Championships for the first time in San Francisco, USA. There are mountain bike racing types that are not recognized by the UCI, such as mountain bike orienteering, that are governed by the IOF.

© olly, 2012. Used under license from Shutterstock, Inc.

Cyclo-Cross

Cyclo-cross is a form of bicycle racing. Races typically take place in the autumn and winter (the international or "World Cup" season is September–January), and consists of many laps of a short (2.5–3.5 km or 1.5–2 mile) course featuring pavement, wooded trails, grass, steep hills, and obstacles requiring the rider to quickly dismount, carry the bike whilst navigating the obstruction and remount. Races for senior categories are generally between 30 minutes and an hour long, with the distance varying depending on the ground conditions. The sport is strongest in the traditional road cycling countries such as Belgium (and Flanders in particular), France, and the Netherlands.

Cyclo-cross has some obvious parallels with mountain bike racing, cross-country cycling, and criterium racing. Many of the best cyclo-cross riders cross-train in other cycling disciplines. However, cyclo-cross has reached such a size and popularity that some racers are specialists, and many never race anything but cyclo-cross races. Cyclo-cross bicycles are similar to racing bicycles: lightweight, with narrow tires and drop handlebars. However, they also share characteristics with mountain bicycles in that they utilize knobby tread tires for traction, and cantilever style brakes for clearance, needed due to muddy conditions. They have to be lightweight because competitors need to carry their bicycle to overcome barriers or slopes too steep to

climb in the saddle. The sight of competitors struggling up a muddy slope with bicycles on their shoulders is the classic image of the sport, although unridable sections are generally a very small fraction of the race distance.

Compared with other forms of cycle racing, tactics are fairly straightforward, and the emphasis is on the rider's aerobic endurance and bike-handling skills. Drafting, where cyclists form a line with the lead cyclist pedaling harder while reducing the wind resistance for other riders, is of much less importance than in road racing, where average speeds are much higher than in cyclo-cross. A cyclo-cross rider is allowed to change bicycles and receive mechanical assistance during a race. While the rider is on the course gumming up one bicycle with mud, his or her pit crew can work quickly to clean, repair, and oil the spares. Having a mechanic in the "pits" is more common for professional cyclo-cross racers. The average cyclo-cross racer might have a family member or friend holding their spare bike.

BICYCLE EVENTS OR TOUR RIDES

Even if you still feel that competing isn't for you, there are plenty of event rides that you might enjoy. During bicycling weather, these rides are held almost every weekend. Events usually offer participants a choice of 10, 25, 50, 75, or 100 mile routes and the events are usually held in conjunction with local or nationwide charities. These events raise money for some very worthy causes. The group hosting the ride will usually have pit stops set up along the route as well as SAG (Support And Gear) support. Sag support is provided by automobiles that follow the riders on the course carrying extra supplies such as wheels, tires, and food. These rides are generally low-key and are great rides for family and friends. In Waco, Texas for example, Skittles holds the "Waco Wild West Century." The event raises money for the National Marrow Donor Program. Whether you like to compete, or just ride, cycling offers something for everyone!

CHAPTER 14

Mountain Biking

Mountain biking is one of the most enjoyable forms of cycling. There are some absolutely amazing trails out there and they come in all skill levels. There are trails that provide an opportunity for you to take a leisurely stroll through the woods to escape the everyday hustle and bustle, and there are trails that will challenge both your physical as well as your technical abilities. Contrary to what many believe, mountain biking is not as dangerous as road biking. You get to pick a trail that suits your skill level and pretty much control the amount of risks you want to take. While riding a road bike, your biggest risks are not controlled by you, but by whoever is behind the wheel of the cars you share the road with.

Mountain biking does require you to take your skill set to another level in order to really enjoy the sport as well as to keep it safe. Below are some core skills, why they are important, and how to practice making them better.

CORE SKILLS

All mountain bike moves that are necessary for successfully riding trails are based on 5 core skills: **perception, balance, braking, steering,** and **pedaling**.

Perception

Perception of how you're going to ride through obstacles basically triggers your moves. Focus on where you want to go and what's in that path. Most beginning mountain bikers tend to look at things they don't want to hit and in doing so, they hit them!

- Ignore what's not in your way and stay focused on where you want to go. Look beyond the obstacle, not at it, or you could be unprepared for what lies just ahead.
- If you can hit obstacles straight on, then do so.
- You can roll over anything that's one-quarter the size of your wheel or less. (5-6 inches on a 26″ bike and 6-7 inches on a 29er). ***Try to keep your crank arms parallel to the ground when riding over obstacles***.
- Your body is independent of your bike so gravity plays a huge role. If your bike comes to a sudden stop…you won't.

GOOD PRACTICE – Walk a section of a trail and make mental notes of the obstacles. Pick the path with the least amount of trouble and ride it. Look only at the path you picked, nothing else.

Balance

Being a good mountain biker is about having good balance and being able to keep that balance when you hit an obstacle. Your legs and your arms serve as your shocks. Let them absorb the impact whenever possible.

- To have good balance on a bike, you need to start with a bike that fits you (see chapter 3).
- Check your posture and make sure your arms are slightly flexed.
- Your center of gravity should fall in the middle of where your two wheels contact the ground. Your center of gravity is basically your heart.
- Use your arms and legs as shock absorbers.
- Generally speaking, your weight should shift back going down a slope and forward going up a slope.
- The crouching position where your weight is slightly back and your arms are flexed bringing your chest closer to the top tube is the base of good riding technique.

GOOD PRACTICE – With the pedals parallel to the ground, practice riding while standing up. This is a great way to start to learn to use your weight in order to stay balanced. Practice this through turns, straightaways, as well as up and down hills. Uphill you will obviously have to pedal, but try doing so standing.

Braking

Learning to use your brakes properly is more important in mountain biking than any other form of cycling. Always be ready to brake, which means keeping at least one finger on the brake lever at all times. I keep one finger on the front brake lever and two fingers on the back break lever.

- When applying the brakes, remember that it will cause your weight to go forward, so be prepared.
- To stop on a flat surface, your brakes have about equal stopping force; going downhill, however, the front wheel has about 95% of the stopping force and the back wheel only has about 5%. This means your front brake is really needed to slow you down (be ready because a sudden squeeze on the front brake lever could send a unsuspecting rider over the handlebars).
- Practice braking both on flats and downhills as well as through corners to get a full understanding of how your brakes react.

GOOD PRACTICE – Practice coming to a stop going down slopes without the tire skidding. First focus more on the back brakes, then again focusing on the front brakes. This should give you a good idea as to how much of each brake to apply and when.

Steering

Even though most of us feel the steering skills we perfected as kids are just fine, those skills will not be sufficient in becoming a successful mountain biker. Working on your ability to steer your bike with more than just your hands will pay huge dividends.

- As stated in the perception section, always look where you want to go.
- Engage the turn with your body.
- Use proper form. The inside pedal should always be up. Push down on the outside pedal and slightly forward on the inside handlebar to cause the bike to lean into the turn.
- Use the straightest path whenever possible.
- A great drill is to practice riding figure 8s.

GOOD PRACTICE – A great way to improve your steering is by riding figure 8s. The tighter the circles, the better. Also practice simple turns using your weight by leaning into the turn with the inside pedal up.

Pedaling

Pedaling is simply about applying power when you need it. To pedal efficiently, you will need a good understanding of how the gears on your bike work as well as how to use them. Using the gears properly allows you to use a sustainable amount of strength. In other words, you can use the same amount of intensity regardless of the amount of slope. When you do need extra power in certain areas, simply get off the saddle. By standing up, it will allow you to use your body weight to push the pedals.

Most mountain bikes have 3 chain rings in the front and 9 cogs in the back allowing for basically 27 gear combinations. Many of these combinations are redundant and a few put you in a cross chain situation. For this reason, I have a 2 x 10 setup on my bike, (2 chain rings in the front and 10 cogs in the rear). Refer to chapter 5 on how gears work.

- The big chain ring on the front works with the 4 smallest cogs on the back.
- The middle chain ring on the front works with all but the largest and smallest cog on the back.
- The small chain ring on the front works with the 4 largest cogs on the back.

GOOD PRACTICE – Pick a less challenging slope and ride it while using your highest gear. Then ride the same slope using your lowest gear. This should give you a feel of what each gear requires of you. Repeat the process on a more difficult slope.

Again, perception plays a huge role in gear selection. If you wait too late to go to a lower or a higher gear, you will put undue stress on both the chain and your legs. This could result in you dropping or even breaking the chain.

© Dudarev Mikhail, 2012. Used under license from Shutterstock, Inc.

MOUNTAIN BIKING CHAPTER TEST

1. What are the 5 core skills needed for mountain biking? _____

    _____

    _____

2. To have good balance on a bike, you need to start with a bike that

    _____ you.

3. When mountain biking, you can roll over anything that is _____ the size of

    your wheel or less.

4. Two good rules of thumb you should follow when steering are to always

    _____ where you want to go and _____ the turn

    with your body.

5. Understanding the _____ on your bike will help you to pedal more

    efficiently.

6. Being a good mountain biker is about having good _____ and being

    able to keep the balance when you hit an _____.

7. When applying the brakes, remember that it will cause your weight to go

    _____ so be prepared.

8. What might happen if you wait too late to go to a lower or higher gear? _____

    _____

    _____

    _____

GLOSSARY

Aero bars – Extensions that stick out in front of the handlebars to allow the rider to get into an aerodynamically low position.

Aero wheels – A wheel designed to reduce wind resistance.

Air – The amount of space between your tires and the ground. The more, the better.

Allen key – A hexagonal tool used to loosen or tighten the majority of the bolts on a bike.

ATB – All-Terrain Biking or Bike. The same as MTB.

Anaerobic threshold – The exercise level where the body begins to switch from aerobic (oxygen-using) to less-efficient anaerobic processes to produce energy.

Anchor bolt – The bolt that fixes brake and/or gear cables into place.

Auger – To take samples of the local terrain, usually with your face, by crashing.

Axle – The shaft around which wheels and cranksets rotate.

Baby heads – Small round rocks on a trail, similar in size to their namesake but more difficult to ride over.

Bail – To part company from your bike in anticipation of crashing.

Barrel adjuster – Threaded attachment on brake or gear units that allows for fine adjusting.

BB – Bottom bracket, the bearing unit around which the crankset rotates.

Bead – One of the two inner edges of a clincher-type tire. It includes a strengthening metal or fiber cable to prevent the air pressure from stretching the tire larger than the rim.

Berm – A banked corner.

Blocking – Legally impeding the progress of riders in the pack to allow teammates in the break a better chance of success.

Bonk – To run out of energy.

Boot – A temporary patch placed on a punctured tire to protect the tube.

Bottle cage – A bracket for holding a water bottle on a bicycle frame.

BPM – Beats Per Minute – the measure of your heart rate.

Brake boss – The mounting point for the brakes.

Brake pad – The replaceable part of the brake that does the slowing down for you.

Brakehoods – The rubber covers over the brake lever mechanism on drop handlebars.

Braze-ons – The threaded pegs on bike frames to attach bottle cages, racks, or other accessories.

Bunny hop – Lifting both wheels off the ground to clear an obstacle.

Bushing – A sleeve used as a bearing on certain forks, pivots, and jockey wheels.

Cable – Braided or twisted wire used to operate brakes and gears.

Cable housing – The sheath that guides the gear and brake cables.

Cadence – The speed of pedaling.

Campy – The nick name for Campagnolo, the premier component manufacturer.

Cantilever brakes – Caliper brakes in which the pivot point is below the rim and attached to the frame or fork.

Cat, Category – The competition level in USCF-sponsored races. Cat 5 = beginner, Cat 4 = novice, Cat 3 = sport, Cat 2 = expert, Cat 1 = elite.

Century – 100 miles, metric century, 100 kilometers or 62 miles.

Chain – A series of links held together by pins; the life-blood of the drive train.

Chain line – An imaginary line that connects the middle chain ring and the middle rear sprocket.

Chain ring – A toothed sprocket attached to a crank arm.

Chain stay – The section of the frame that connects the BB and the rear dropouts.

Chain suck – When the chain gets caught between the granny ring and the frame, often in muddy conditions and often when the chain and/or the chain rings are worn.

Chain whip – A tool used to remove sprockets.

Clean – To make it through a technical section without dabbing.

Cleat – The mechanism on the bottom of a bicycle shoe that locks into a clipless pedal.

Clincher – The standard wire or Kevlar beaded tire.

Clipless pedal – Pedals where the shoes engage via cleats, creating a firm bond that is released by twisting the heel outwards.

Cog – Toothed sprocket on the rear hub.

Compression damping – A setting to control the speed of absorption of the impact a bump makes on a shock's spring.

Computer – A cyclocomputer.

Crank arm – The levers of a crankset that you turn with the pedals.

Crankset – A unit comprising BB, crank arms and chain rings.

Criterium (Crit) – A bike race that goes around many laps on a short course.

Cross-country – The most common form of racing.

Dab – To put a foot on the ground in a technical section.

Damper – The unit in a shock that determines the rate of compression.

Damping – The controlled absorption of the compression of a shock.

Death cookies – Fist-size rocks on a trail that point you and your bike everywhere except where you are planning on going.

Derailleur – The device that shifts the chain over sprockets or chain rings.

Derailleur hanger – The part of the frame where the rear derailleur bolts on; usually replaceable due to its vulnerability.

Dialed in – This describes a bike that fits perfectly or a ride or race that was perfect.

Dish – The offsetting of the rear right side spokes to allow room for the cassette.

Disk brake – An automotive-style braking system that has brakes working on disks attached to the hub, rather than the conventional rim brakes.

Down tube – The frame tube that connects the head tube to the bottom bracket.

Draft – Riding in the slipstream of the rider ahead.

Drivetrain – The chain, BB, cranks, chain rings, sprockets, and derailleurs.

Dropouts – The slots in the fork and chain stays where the wheels clamp in.

Drops – The lower part of the drop-style handlebars.

Endo – Flying over the front handlebars while the bike goes end-over-end.

Face plant – When the rider's face hits the ground after an endo.

Fit kit – A set of measuring tools that bike shops use to optimize bike fit.

Fixed gear (fixie) – A single gear bike with no coaster mechanism.

Float – The amount of foot rotation available on a clipless pedal.

Grade – The steepness of a hill, measured in percent. Equal to feet of vertical rise per hundred feet of horizontal distance.

Granny gear – The lowest gear on the bike, the one your granny would need on all but the flattest roads, and you need on the steepest.

Granny ring – The smallest chain ring. See granny gear.

GripShift – Gear shifters that are part of the handlebar grip, change gear by twisting.

Gruppo – A complete set of components by the same manufacturer.

Hammer (or mash) – To ride hard in a high gear.

Hammer-head – A rider who only knows how to ride hard.

Hardtail – A mountain bike with no rear suspension.

Headset – The bearing unit around which your steering rotates.

Head tube – The frame tube that supports the steer tube, and thus the fork.

Hydraulic brake – A powerful braking system, usually disk that uses hydraulic oil instead of cables.

Hood – Brake hood.

JRA – Just Riding Along; the preamble for virtually every rider-caused trip to the bike shop. Usually used when looking for warranty replacement.

Knobbies – Typical off-road tires, with deeply molded treads for better grip.

LBS – Local Bike Shop

Line – The best route through any section of trail.

MTB – Mountain Biking or Bike

Masterlink – A special chain link that is used to break the chain rather than pushing out a rivet.

Nipple – The threaded nut that tightens spokes.

Peleton – The main group of cyclists in a race.

Pinch flat – A flat caused by getting the tube caught between the rim and a rock.

Presta valve – Also known as racing valve, the thinner and more user-friendly tube valve available…see Schrader valve.

PSI – Pounds per Square Inch, the accepted unit of pressure when pumping up tires.

Quick release brakes – Brakes with provision to easily open up the calipers for quick wheel removal.

Quick release levers – A lever used on wheel hubs, and sometimes seat posts, which replaces the locknut for easy, no-tool removal or adjustment.

Rapidfire – Shimano's most successful shifting system.

Rebound damping – The rate of return-to-normal a shock spring possesses.

Rim – The outer ring of the wheel, to which the tire is fitted.

Roadie – A cyclist who has not yet embraced mountain biking.

Road rash – The wound resulting from flesh dragged across a road surface.

Rollers – A type of training stand in which the rider must maintain balance to keep the bicycle upright.

Saddle – The instrument of torture that connects our rear ends to the bike.

Saddle sore –An abrasion, boil, or pressure sore caused by contact with the saddle.

SAG wagon – A vehicle that follows a group of riders to pick up those who need assistance.

Schrader valve – Also known as car valve. See Presta valve.

Seat post – The removable tube that the saddle mounts onto.

Seat stays – The tubes that connect the rear wheel to the top of the seat tube.

Seat tube – The frame tube that connects between the top tube and the

bottom bracket. The seat post inserts into the top of the seat tube.

Singletrack – Nirvana for mountain bikers; a trail wide enough for just one bike.

Skewer – The quick release mechanism that holds the wheels on.

Snake bite – See pinch flat.

Spider – The right crank arm without its chain rings.

Spider patrol – The first rider to ride a trail in the moring, clearing cobwebs as he goes.

Spin – To maintain a high cadence.

Spoke – The tensioned wire that connects the rim to the hub, completing the wheel.

Sprockets – The rear cogs.

Squirrel – A rider who cannot maintain a straight line or is unpredictable.

Stand over – The amount of clearance between the top tube of the bike and your nether regions when you stop.

Steer tube, steerer, steering tube – The tube that goes through the head tube and connects the fork to the handlebar stem.

Stage race – A race in which a different course is traversed each day. The winner is the racer with the lowest total time.

Stem – The tube that connects the handlebars to the steer tube.

Switchback – A tight corner that covers almost 180 degrees.

Taco (pretzel or potato chip) – To bend a wheel.

Technical – A trail or route that requires a high level of skill to traverse.

Time trial – A bicycle race in which cyclists race against the clock rather than directly against each other. Racers start set times apart and are prohibited from drafting each other.

Top tube – The top, horizontal frame member that connects between the head tube and the seat tube.

Tops – The part of the handlebar between the stem and the brake levers.

Touring bike – Compared with a standard road bike, a touring bike frame is sturdier, more extended, has relaxed frame geometry and clearance, and braze-ons for fenders and racks.

Track stand – Balancing the bike while still with both feet on the pedals.

Trainer, training stand – A frame that converts a bicycle into an exercise (stationary) bicycle. Allows training indoors in bad weather.

Travel – The maximum length of movement on a suspension system.

USCF – United States Cycling Federation. Sanctions bicycle races.

Velodrome – A bicycle racing track, usually with steeply banked curves.

VO$_2$ max – A person's maximum oxygen intake rate.

Wash out – When one or both wheels slide out from under you.

Wheelbase – The distance between the front and back axles.

Wheelie – To ride on the back wheel only.

Work stand, or repair stand – A frame that holds a bicycle off the ground for convenient repair.

700C – A wheel size used on road bikes of approximately 700 mm (27.6 inch) diameter, including tire.

29er – A mountain bike that uses 29 inch wheels as opposed to 26 inch wheels.

USEFUL WEBSITES

International Cycling Union (UCI)   www.uci.ch

USA Cycling   www.usacycling.org

Bicycling Info Center   www.bicyclinginfo.org

Bike Radar   www.bikeradar.com

Bike Reg   www.bikereg.com